UNIVERSITY OF NOTTINGHAM

1002183902

WITH

FROM T.

D0265319

# Marketing in Context

# MARKETING IN CONTEXT

## Setting the Scene

Chris Hackley

BUSINESS LIBRARY

palgrave
macmillan

© Chris Hackley 2013

All rights reserved. No reproduction, copy or transmission of this publication may be made without written permission.

No portion of this publication may be reproduced, copied or transmitted save with written permission or in accordance with the provisions of the Copyright, Designs and Patents Act 1988, or under the terms of any licence permitting limited copying issued by the Copyright Licensing Agency, Saffron House, 6-10 Kirby Street, London EC1N 8TS.

Any person who does any unauthorized act in relation to this publication may be liable to criminal prosecution and civil claims for damages.

The author has asserted his right to be identified as the author of this work in accordance with the Copyright, Designs and Patents Act 1988.

First published 2013 by
PALGRAVE MACMILLAN

Palgrave Macmillan in the UK is an imprint of Macmillan Publishers Limited, registered in England, company number 785998, of Houndmills, Basingstoke, Hampshire RG21 6XS.

Palgrave Macmillan in the US is a division of St Martin's Press LLC, 175 Fifth Avenue, New York, NY 10010.
1007283502
Palgrave Macmillan is the global academic imprint of the above companies and has companies and representatives throughout the world.

Palgrave® and Macmillan® are registered trademarks in the United States, the United Kingdom, Europe and other countries

ISBN: 978-1-137-29710-5

This book is printed on paper suitable for recycling and made from fully managed and sustained forest sources. Logging, pulping and manufacturing processes are expected to conform to the environmental regulations of the country of origin.

A catalogue record for this book is available from the British Library.

A catalog record for this book is available from the Library of Congress.

*I dedicate this book to my wife Amy Rungpaka, my daughter Dulcie-Bella Caitlin and my sons Michael, James and Nicholas*

# Contents

# Contents

# CHAPTER 1

# Setting the Marketing Scene

## MARKETING AND ITS CONTEXT

Marketing is many things to many people, and our view of it is framed by the contexts in which we encounter it. For critics, marketing is a field of thought and practice that has become closely identified with humbug and hyperbole.[1] We might have an enduring fascination with the way it tantalizes us with fantasies of self-realization, but in general, marketing receives a bad press for its trite theories, its impudent techniques, and its tendency to sneak uninvited into every corner of life. In the developed world, we could hardly deny that marketing has contributed to a level of material affluence that our grandparents would have thought utterly enviable. Yet, few of us would say that it makes us happier or more fulfilled, and our attempts to understand how marketing really works are patchy, at best. Even for the marketing cognoscenti, the state of the field seems poorly articulated. Marketing's "how-to" management books offer characteristically underargued and overgeneralized prescriptions, typically juxtaposed with carefully edited, but "so-what?" case examples. Academics don't do much better – marketing's academic researchers produce huge volumes of esoteric findings that rarely seem to connect with the everyday priorities of managers and consumers. More often than not, stand-out marketing innovations simply don't seem to fit conventional text book explanations. All in all, marketing is a huge economic and cultural presence with far reaching implications for us all, yet we still don't understand nearly enough about this familiar yet enigmatic subject.

I'm interested in another way of understanding marketing, not as a set of formulaic management techniques, or as a deep science of consumer control, but as something that is produced by, and experienced in, particular social situations. Marketing in practice has a social texture, in its workplaces, its consumption experiences, and also in its unintended effects. In this book I want to explore the idea that this social texture, the fine detail and relational dynamics of situations, the *context* for marketing, can be treated as a connecting principle. I maintain that context is what gives meaning to marketing issues and situations, so an appreciation of context can be the fabric that links different marketing situations together. My guiding metaphor for the contextual approach to marketing is the mise-en-scéne, a concept from film criticism that I'll say more about below. The book develops the contextual approach as a way of doing, as well as analyzing, marketing, with relevance to marketing practice, management education and consumer policy.

By the marketing context, I mean everything and anything that occupies the marketing landscape. This might include things that are visual, aural, psychological, textual, implicit or explicit, physiological, cultural, sensual, symbolic or material. That is, the entire cultural and material context in which marketing operates, and through which consumers move. I think marketing, broadly conceived, frames and penetrates our experiences of everyday life to quite an extent. Seen in this light, the job of marketing is to set the scene in such a way as to activate our emotions and engage consumer passions. For practitioners, I argue that sensitivity to context can be cultivated as an intellectual trait, and incorporated into management systems. I see contextual marketing thinking as fluid and holistic, boundary-spanning, creative, and communication-focused. I contend that typical business school theory routinely fails to account for the contexts in which we encounter marketing, because of an over-reliance on instrumental techniques and reductionist cause-effect approaches, what I call cue-ball theories of marketing. There is a concomitant tendency in management education to take an outside-in, client-side approach to marketing, instead of trying to reveal its inner workings from the perspective of marketing's expert practitioners.

There are plenty of people who claim to be experts retailing their anecdotes in academic settings, and personal stories certainly have an educational value. But, I think the anecdotal approach has a major failing. People who really are experts are often not very good at explaining what they do or how they do it. Their skills are often intuitive, and based on experience and pragmatic problem solving. For them, there is nothing much to say about doing marketing, but to work hard, learn from experience, and know your business inside-out. The value of the academic perspective lies not in trying to mimic the way experts talk, but in finding ways to articulate their practical experience, and in analyzing the ways in which their practice plays out. I will try to illustrate in the book how an appreciation of consumer cultural context offers a richer and more useful account of marketing effects that informs both the practical management of marketing, and the understanding of its effects, both intended and not.

The contextual approach considers marketing issues in terms of a Gestalt, a totality, comprising interdependent parts moving within a system. Imagine walking through the Las Vegas Strip at night, every viewing angle filled with neon spectacle. As a mise-en-scéne, the strip might not be subtle, but it is a total environment that has a way of luring you into the Vegas spirit of consumption, and sucking the money out of your pockets with an invisible force. This is how I conceive consumption contexts, as spatial environments that are crafted, to some extent, as spectacle, with a persuasive intent. You could swap Las Vegas for a small market town, or your living room, and the principle is the same. Marketing, in part, is the art of setting the consumer scene to enthrall and persuade, and framing the contexts of consumption experiences.

The idea of taking in the full context of consumption is unorthodox partly because organizations and professions, and their counterparts in university departments, operate within disciplinary silos, which reduce the scope of marketing to fit into their own ideologies and language-games. These artificial sub-divisions often fail to connect with each other, or with the experiential worlds of marketing. A contextual approach demands connection and linkage. Marketing professionals who try to operate at a connected level that takes in the whole context have a good deal of work to do to build internal trust, establish networks, and nurture boundary-crossing working relationships because of these disciplinary silos. I hope to highlight practical ways in which marketing professionals might generate and communicate the insights of a contextual understanding. I also want to sketch out a view of marketing as an educational discipline that builds students' knowledge and intellectual skills not by playing on a simplistic, one-dimensional view of the world, replete with static marketing concepts and cue-ball notions of cause and effect, but by acknowledging the complex socio-cultural context of marketing and consumption. This, I hope, can contribute to a richer, more effective, and more intellectually viable discipline.

## TALKING MARKETING

I will touch on some of the theoretical issues around this contextual approach to marketing practice as the book progresses, but as far as possible I want to describe its implications in everyday language. I've found in my many conversations with expert practitioners in marketing that these professionals tend to eschew technical language and management jargon in favor of a contingent, nuanced, and fluid style of talking about their experience of doing marketing.[2] There is sometimes a place for technical jargon, to be sure. As an academic, I have a particular weakness for the esoteric vocabulary of social science, but I think the use of non-technical language is a virtue and I will try to convey the notion of contextual marketing with that in mind. Just because the way expert practitioners talk about their work may be prosaic, though, doesn't mean their grasp of marketing is unsophisticated. Far from it. I feel that although many experts use ordinary language to talk about their work, their thinking often rests on implicit assumptions that unconsciously reflect aspects of social scientific method. For example, there are often implicit positions taken on the nature of social life, the most appropriate methods of understanding it, the ways agency and structure can play out in consumption, and the best ways to use human insights to strategize and make meaningful connections with people. These practitioners *do* marketing by applying informal social scientific thinking, but not in a rigid or prescriptive way. They deploy implicit theories to apply to their everyday work[3] and these theories help them to act creatively to respond to the particular context of each situation. The best analogy I've found for this contextual approach lies in the account planning role in advertising,[4] but the principle of expert ordinary language applies, in my view, to any marketing role that demands strategic thinking.

In top advertising agencies around the world, I've asked senior account team professionals how they created their most striking, successful, and award-winning advertising. Advertising, perhaps above other marketing industries, has had to adapt to the new, convergent marketing landscape, and it sits at the apex of new, communication-based branding and business models. Generating the consumer and marketing insights to feed into communication and marketing strategy takes intellectual poise, fluency of linguistic expression, sensitivity to data, imagination, openness and, perhaps above all, an ability to take in the Gestalt, the context of marketing. The ways a given marketing intervention could affect the constituent parts and relationships of a particular marketing context need to be finely judged, articulated, debated, and acted upon. The focus has to shift from the particulars of a given situation to the broader cultural context and back again, and the new knowledge has to be assimilated into evolving strategies.

## MARKETING'S PLACE IN THE WORLD

I'm not suggesting that marketing practitioners are philosopher-kings benignly exercising their wisdom for the good of you, me, and the world. Let's be honest, the mystique of marketing practice owes much to mystification, and the field employs generous helpings of delusion and deceit, not to mention more than a touch of narcissism and native cunning. There are mistakes, accidents, cock-ups and catastrophes, and dollops of try-it-and-see, often followed closely by a surfeit of being-smart-after-the-event. Much marketing is prosaic and pedestrian, and decidedly low concept. One of the many contradictions of marketing is that years of blowing its own trumpet may have made a very loud noise, but its PR is pretty awful. Marketing occupies a deeply contradictory place in the world. It remains a boom subject in business studies, with many hundreds of thousands of students studying it in schools, colleges, universities, and with professional associations around the world. Yet marketing, and those who practice this not-quite-but-almost dark art, are regarded with contempt by many, as a bad joke by some, and as a cause of much that is worst about the world by others. Marketing is blamed for all manner of social ills, and its exponents are stereotyped as cynical manipulators. Those who write marketing books for managers are sometimes thought an even lower species, parasitically feeding off marketing's rotten corpse. Burp.

On the other hand, most of us can agree, after a little prompting, that marketing is much more congenial than the alternative – state planning. What is more, it is far too important not to be written about. If pushed, most people would even agree that they enjoy having different stuff to choose from when they shop, and that advertising and promotion can add color to the world of consumption, when they're done well. Some might even accept that most organizations have to engage with markets, however that is conceived, hence a marketing discipline is economically necessary. There is less agreement when we consider what kind or what quantity of marketing we want, and when we start to wonder what forms of marketing genuinely serve consumer sovereignty and organizational efficiency, or undermine them. I take the view that a better understanding of marketing ought to benefit not only practitioners and business, but citizens too. The place to start is to think about marketing in a different way, and to dispense with its reified categories and arthritic theories in favor of a lighter but more penetrating approach. With this lofty thought in mind, the book tries to explore and explain the holistic, contextual, and fluid way of understanding marketing that I believe is practiced by many of its finest exponents, and which might well offer the best explanations of many of its most interesting manifestations.

## THE MISE-EN-SCÉNE

The metaphor that inspired this book comes, unexpectedly, from film criticism. It is the concept of the mise-en-scéne, which was first applied to theatre and became extended to film criticism. My simplistic[5] sense of it is that it illustrates something important about the kind of marketing practice I have seen and that I most admire, the kind that I don't find explained or even acknowledged in typical marketing text books and theories. Mise-en-scéne is a French term that literally means something like "to place in the scene", but its role in film criticism is both more nebulous and more significant than mere set dressing. It refers to the ways in which the physical space of a theatre stage, or a film set, can be used to tell the story by conveying nuances of emotion, aspects of characterization or plot, or other elements of storytelling. It is most commonly associated with film scenes that linger for some time on one set, and its effect derives from the careful arrangement of light, actors, cinematography, depth of field, scenery, costume, script, "blocking" or positioning of actors, actors' gestures, and also sound, not as individual elements but as a Gestalt that distils and conveys meaning in dynamic interaction. One example is a scene early in the 2004 film *The Libertine*, starring Johnny Depp as the Earl of Rochester, in which the camera spins slowly around to take a lingering, in-the-round view of a raucus London theatre. Sound is sometimes excluded from the idea of mise-en-scéne, but some film critics include it where the sound is diegetic, that is, where it evolves from within the scene and plays a role in telling the story. Mise-en-scéne is a composition of light, color, camera movement and set design, framing and filling a cinematographic space that can be potentially open, or closed and self-contained. The mise-en-scéne is primarily about the way space is utilized and it allows the viewer to look around and find things, rather than directing the viewer's attention closely through rapid editing. Although mainly a visual concept, the music, sound, script and acting can be complimentary to the mise-en-scéne effect. I see mise-en-scéne as a concept that captures something important but neglected in contemporary marketing. Its aim is to activate the viewer, to generate a response, to elicit emotional engagement. These aims also happen to be the cornerstones of contemporary marketing.

By implication, in order to be able to play with the senses and emotions of the viewer, the movie director has to intimately understand the audience and its social milieu, as well as the craft of movie making. I see the mise-en-scéne as referring in part to the way a film director will tell a complex story with powerful economy, using all the aspects of the scene. In this book I take some liberties with the mise-en-scéne metaphor, since marketing situations tend to be in a continuous flux, while a film set is static, at least until the director starts the action. In addition, film or theatre audiences generally have one perspective since they are static, whereas consumers often move through marketing sets. We experience scenes as static observers when we, say, watch TV at home, go to the cinema, or read a magazine. We respond to these scenes as an audience. We also experience scenes as we move through them, say, when we walk through shopping malls, or when we view TV, mobile phone and notebook screens in quick sequence; we might travel by car through urban spaces, walk from one restaurant to another in a city centre, or experience a theme park or servicescape. The metaphor holds, though, whether the viewer is static or in motion, in the sense that we experience and respond emotionally to the scenes we encounter.

There are also many differences between the theatrical mise-en-scéne and the marketing scene. For example, the film director is in absolute control of all the elements of the set. The marketing professional, in contrast, might have control over one or two elements of the marketing scene, at most. What I bring from the metaphor is the understanding of marketing that can derive from a careful analysis of all the elements of the consumer scene in inter-action, in engagement with the audience. This does not imply that the consumer is an unwitting dupe under the control of environmental psychology – we may respond to environmental cues but, as any shop merchandiser, window-dresser, or store designer will tell you, humans do not respond in a mechanistic way to external stimuli. We may not respond at all. To activate the consumer requires an understanding of the sensibility of consumers in engagement with marketing, as well as a detailed appreciation of the scene in which that engagement will take place.

Some people would probably regard my analogy between marketing and drama as preposterous. Drama, as art, is seen as sacred, since it can have a moral value, while marketing is profane, since it activates only one emotion: greed. But I would not see it so starkly. Marketing is deeply integrated into popular culture, and it is increasingly difficult to see where marketing ends and popular culture begins. Some might see the merger of marketing and branding with enter-tainment and mass communication, as an exploitative culture industry[6] designed not to activate audiences, but to sedate them. I'd argue that marketing fails to achieve the degree of manipulative control that is often claimed for it. It borrows popular art and culture not to dictate cultural meaning but to create spaces for creative, postmodern interpretation. I'm not suggesting that all marketing is like this, but that much of the best and most interesting work in marketing does operate in this way. I don't see this as a dismal statement on the poverty of our cultural life under neo-liberal capitalism, but as a rich and intriguing source of insight about the ways we respond as consumers to our environments. The mise-en-scéne is a way of imagining the dynamism and theatricality of marketing situations that have the potential to activate, engage, and involve audiences by using any combination of elements in the sensory environment. I also like the analogy for the space the mise-en-scéne gives to an audience to think, to interpret, and perhaps to resist, reject, or walk away. The idea of an active, interpreting consumer contrasts with the dreary cognitivism and behaviorism that blight so much marketing. In film theory, the mise-en-scéne is associated with long, artful scenes, sometimes using a tracking shot to follow the actors. This is contrasted with the more common ABC (Always Be Cutting) approach to movie making which leaves the viewer with less room for interpretation and directs their attention more actively. The quintessential mise-en-scéne example is the eight-minute, uncut opening shot of Robert Altman's Hollywood satire *The Player.* Such a long scene is based on the assumption that the audience possess the attention span and the intelligence to assimilate a great deal of information in a short time. My contention is that the most creative and most effective marketing applies similar principles in granting the audience the interpretive space to engage with marketing scenes in ways that may be suggested, perhaps framed, but are not controlled. I see the consumer responding to marketing scenes not necessarily with a hegemonic reading, uncritically accepting the meaning encoded by the sender, but with room for resistance or re-interpretation.

Marketing is much less than a science of consumer control, despite its often outlandish claims. Nonetheless, seen as a cultural force that is often implicitly persuasive, its influence is profound. The better it is understood, the better marketing can serve everyone. I'd like now to begin to try to give some substance to the contextual perspective with a well-known story about a piece of opportunistic marketing action that, although unorthodox, does seem, to me, to carry some wider lessons about the importance of understanding context for marketing practice today.

## THE OLYMPIC CHEEK OF DR DRE

This story caught my eye, along with millions of others, during the London 2012 Olympics. The International Olympic Committee (IOC) had made it clear that only official sponsors could be associated with the games in any way. For a few days, though, Dr Dre managed to make the Olympic swimming events an exclusive, free, product placement vehicle for his *Beats* headphones. Product placement, for the uninitiated, refers to the presence of a brand in the scene, script, or plot of an entertainment vehicle. The exposure of Dr Dre's headphones in the context of TV coverage of the London Olympics had prominence, plot congruency, celebrity leverage, and tie-in with other media comment. Suffice to say, the product placement in the *James Bond* movie *Skyfall* looked understated by comparison. The difference was that this one cost Dr Dre nothing.

It wasn't an entirely new stunt – it was reported that at the 2008 Beijing Olympics *Beats* headphones were given to American Basketball star LeBron James who passed them out to other team members. But the London Olympic organizing committee, called Logoc, had made their intention to block ambush marketers very public indeed. London 2012 was a hugely successful sports sponsorship venture with brands including *McDonald's, Coca Cola, BMW, Samsung, Omega*, and *P&G* paying up to a reported £65 million each to be top tier sponsors while supplying products and services too. Logoc wanted to protect these investments and ambush marketers were in their sights. It was even rumored that small local shops in East London were threatened with legal action for daring to dress their windows in anything resembling the Olympic rings. But as the swimmers slouched out of their changing rooms into the spectacular pool venue, with thousands cheering and a billion more watching on TV, it gradually dawned on viewers that most of the headsets worn to block out the crowd noise bore the same distinctive logo. Someone in Dr Dre's organization had apparently noticed that the swimmers were very fond of wearing headphones almost until the starting pistol fired. Dr Dre's rep had kindly handed out free product to competitors. *Beats* headphones are expensive, at upwards of $150, and few athletes get rich swimming, so the gift was received gratefully. Gold plated, top category, 5-star placement ensued, and on the non-commercial BBC to boot.

This exposure fitted the street credibility of the brand like a glove, and the association with cool, young, multinational athletes was clearly just what the Dr ordered. But post hoc logic doesn't do justice to the richness of this example of contextualized marketing. The target audience for *Beats* is, of course, young and cool, like the swimmers. Far too cool to be swayed by conventional advertising. Brands pay top Dollar for sports sponsorship because of its unrivalled reach and symbolic force. Sports events are the last big media audience platform, and the Olympics is the Daddy, even making the American Superbowl and its 100 million viewers look like a school sports day in terms of marketing heft.

Making this exposure even more priceless was the fact that the BBC doesn't sell placements, or advertising, to anyone. It's the world's biggest non-commercial public service broadcaster, although it does sell its TV shows around the world through its commercial arm. Even the paying sponsors had to obey strict rules about how their logos could be displayed. The audience was even bigger than the reported real time worldwide audience of up to a billion, because of re-runs, recordings, DVDs and internet clips. What is more, the media coverage of Dr Dre's crafty re-branding of the Olympic swimming finals played up a key element of the brand positioning of many fashion and music brands – transgression, the breaking of rules. Since Marlon Brando and Elvis Presley, media representations of being young and cool are also intrinsically about the transgression of social norms, defying officialdom and sticking two fingers (or one finger, for Americans) up at convention. What could be cooler for a cool brand than a promotion that was against the rules of promotion?

Dr Dre wasn't the only brand that thumbed its nose at the IOC and Logoc in 2012 – Nike, for example, aired a cheeky parallel campaign featuring towns around the world called "London". But for sheer chutzpah, the Dr Dre ambush takes some beating. Rap and hip pop music is usually about defiance, and Dr Dre's marketing fitted like one of his softly padded head sets. The exposure was perfectly in tune with the soft sell logic of contemporary consumer marketing. It's all about getting the brand embedded in media content with the right audience reach and penetration. If advertising was ever just "salesmanship in print", which I doubt, with great respect to the ad man who invented that enduring aphorism, John E. Kennedy, it is no longer. Get the brand symbolism right in the right media content and sales follow like night follows day, provided the rest of the marketing infrastructure of production, distribution and retail is in place.

Surreptitious product placement, ambush marketing, even guerrilla marketing, call it what you will. The stunt delivered Dr Dre's Beats into living rooms around the world in a way that was unobtrusive, amusing and suggestively powerful. I know nothing of the planning behind this slick and underhand marketing exercise – perhaps it was months or years in the making. Certainly, by all accounts, Dr Dre's headphones operation is fastidiously planned and ruthlessly executed, but I'd guess that, like most marketing practice, there was also a seat-of-the-pants element of "let's try this". In effect, the appearance of the brand in the Olympic swimming finals took an existing cultural norm for many young people, that is, wearing headphones in the presence of other people – rudeness, as it might have once been called – and amplified it by setting it within a scene replete with celebrity sportspeople on the biggest sports marketing platform known to man, the summer Olympics. An understanding of the *context* facilitated a powerful and opportunistic marketing effect that was implicit yet compelling, tacitly connoting transgressive fun, irreverence, coolness, prestige and success.

Product, price, place of distribution, promotion, the tired old marketing mix of standard textbooks, has some relevance in talking about this tricky tale of marketing mischief. The headsets have a visually distinctive design, they are easily recognized and they're well known for their high fidelity in mainlining the most appalling musical form known to mankind – rap – directly into teenage eardrums. What transpired was ineluctably a promotion, of sorts, and hence, it kind of fits into the Four Ps (Product, Price, Promotion and Place of distribution) cliché. But the marketing mix elements were necessary to the ambush effect, not sufficient for it. The mix offers a list of the features of marketing, but it explains nothing about how marketing effects occur in their cultural context. The context that gives meaning and dynamism to any social phenomenon cannot be captured by the static abstractions of text book marketing. The whole context, in its unique inter-action, had to be understood to fully appreciate the way that this exposure was able to leverage such an astronomical amount of free publicity and brand street-kudos.

I am of course, judging the work, and not the outcome. I do not know whether Dr Dre sales figures spiked just after the Olympics (although I do know that my youngest son simply had to have a pair). But, I contend, that would be beside the point for our purposes in understanding marketing in its context. It would be easy to put this example in a box marked marketing communication, ambush, product placement, or another, and bracket it away from general marketing management principles. Yet it embodies the principles of spontaneity, pragmatism, and contextual understanding that underpin so many successful marketing initiatives in a convergent media environment. Almost any consumer brand marketing initiative now leaks across media platforms, garnering instant comment on trade and social media, video responses, parodies, and comment on the comment. This kind of social media reflex is the tiger that planned and paid-for marketing has by the tail. So how might the appreciation of context link back into the common vocabulary and conventional priorities of marketing management? We can begin to explore this by rehearsing conventional ideas about what marketing is supposed to do.

## MARKETING MYTHS

Lay audiences tend to respond to this question with answers like "making money", identifying marketing with one of its sub-disciplines (usually advertising and promotion) or offering a cynical view around the theme "manipulating people to buy stuff they don't need". The vox pop seldom elicits views that marketing increases consumer choice, creates wealth and jobs, sustains organizations or generally makes life much easier and more fun. Marketing does all those things, and, as I maintained earlier, it is better at them than central state planners. Nonetheless, marketing's public image is poor, and many people regard it as a source of cynical manipulation. Within organizations there tends to be a similar division between the neutrals and the skeptics. Marketing advocates in organizations have a tough job in maintaining credibility and arguing for their cause. But the ambivalence, at best, with which marketing is received as a profession, as a knowledge-based discipline, and as a set of dubious techniques for behavioral control, seems at odds with our continuing fascination for it. Marketing education continues to recruit students[7] by the thousand and the discipline enjoys a high-visibility profile. There is near-universal agreement amongst organizations and governments that marketing, whatever is meant by that word, is very important.

Marketing is often seen as the management discipline that delivers pragmatic, behaviorally focused solutions to business problems. Much has been written and said lately of behavioral economics[8] as a discipline that specializes in manipulating citizens' behavior in a policy context, but it is marketing that has long been seen as the quintessential quick fix, one-stop-shop providing tomorrow's customer-oriented solutions today, and remains so. Marketing, we are often told, constantly makes us spend more money than we'd like to, buy stuff we don't really need, and eat things that are bad for us. How it does this is still under discussion. Practitioners in marketing, though, feel much less powerful than their public image as Magi of manipulation would suggest. They usually face a lot of competition, and limits on their resources, and consumers are, actually, very difficult to influence. Many marketing professionals feel that they operate under conditions made ever more difficult by an excess of rules and regulations. Marketing critics point to the supposed Orwellian power marketing, as a whole, wields in propagandizing for a consumer lifestyle, but most marketing practice is carried out in relatively small organizations working at a local level. From the point of view of marketing professionals, talk about the manipulative power of marketing is glib. They feel they're working against cultural forces that are bigger even than Nike or Google.

Marketing's methods, though, are often less impressive than its Big Brother image might suggest. Marketing experts might understand the notion of randomized control trials so beloved of behavioral economics, but everyday marketing practice is often seat-of-the-pants stuff. It's driven not so much by sophisticated-sounding methods of gathering and interpreting statistical evidence to inform well-planned and carefully conceived strategies, but by experiential understanding, and informed commonsense. This common-sense becomes uncommon because of the acute contextual understanding of marketing particulars that it entails. Marketers sometimes have the reputation of being fly, but they are often perceptive, articulate, interested in people, and connected to contemporary cultural trends and mores. Consequently, they can often have a keenly nuanced sense of the contexts of consumer behavior.

My understanding of marketing as a business function is that it should be able to ground the organization in the everyday concerns of consumers, connecting high-minded boardroom strategy with the quotidian lives of people like you and me: the consumers. This is one way of viewing the "marketing concept", the idea that marketing is a mini-philosophy of organizational purpose. Marketing orients organizations toward the external stakeholders who, ultimately, they are supposed to serve. To adapt an axiom from advertising, marketing can provide the voice of the consumer in the organization. At least, that's the idea of the marketing concept. But marketing's mystique, the potential of its techniques to provide a radical and swift transformation of business fortunes, often obscures the contextual specif-icity of the very best marketing strategies. Organizations of every hue frequently act as if a glossy brochure, an expensive advertising campaign, a new product development program, a sales training initiative, a corporate rebranding program, a social media strategy, a new logo, a new marketing strategy, and countless other marketing panaceas, are all that stand between the organization and the eternal bliss of perpetually satisfied customers. All these techniques can have a value, but only if they are applied with a nuanced understanding of the particular context. Marketing techniques are not blunt instruments that will serve organizations in themselves: their effectiveness invariably depends on how their deployment fits the context.

Just occasionally, marketing's big guns do seem to have an elephant gun effect. I still show my advertising students

Bartle Bogle Hegarty's[9] *Levi 501*'s Laundrette ad from the mid 1980s, the ad that increased demand not only for Levi's but for all denim jeans by 800%, or so it was claimed. So, some of my classroom examples may have a barnacle or two stuck to them but the salience remains. Marketing initiatives can sometimes barrel through consumer culture like a rogue rhino through a two man tent, but, much more often, they simply lack the resonance. Marketing is too often conceived in terms of its supposedly forceful techniques, while the importance of sensitivity to the consumer context is forgotten. *Laundrette*, BBH's marquee advertisement of the era, masterfully captivated audiences by tapping into the uniquely powerful provenance of 1950s American popular culture. The ad evinced the teen angst movies of the 1950s. It was a powerful mise-en-scéne packed with evocative American memorabilia that symbolized an American myth, with the sexy teenage rebel, played in the ad by actor Nick Kamen, at centre stage. The atmosphere was framed with the Marvin Gaye soundtrack *I Heard It Through The Grapevine*. Advertising, movies and popular music joined in a sweaty and compelling embrace.[10] Millions of 501s jived off the shelves.

Way back in the 1990s, when I showed my students this ad and asked them to explain the cultural meaning of denim jeans, they talked about the connotations of rebellion, sex, and youth epitomized by James Dean (you won't remember him, don't worry, I'm old). When I showed the ad, the rapt attention of the audience would be palpable. It was a piece of engrossing drama that spoke powerfully to a young audience. A decade later, the ad was viewed by my students as a historical curiosity, and the answers had changed. Denim jeans meant nothing more American than informality. The cultural meaning of denim jeans had lost its frisson of transgression, American provenance had lost some of its prestige, and the jeans market shrunk, and ripped apart, rather like the jeans. Tight jeans had become denuded of any Hollywood-esque sense of youthful rebellion and, instead, were worn, ironed and creased, with shiny shoes and a collared shirt, by bankers weekending at the rugby. They were still popular, and they were still sexy on the right person, but they had lost a unified sense of cultural meaning. The market had fragmented into multiple different cuts, styles, and brands. Cultural meanings, linked with such things as movies, country-of-origin provenance and celebrity icons, change over time, and a key part of the role of marketing is to track these changes, to translate them into organizational action, and also to know when they have changed and it's time to move on. *Laundrette*[11] captured something of a mythical 1950s America that resonated with the world in 1985, but its time eventually passed. The cultural context changed and the iconic symbols of 1950s America lost their force. Laundrette, like the Dr Dre-be-decked swimming scenes of London 2012, was a powerful mise-en-scéne the construction of which required a deep and fluid understanding of the wider cultural context.

## THE SPREAD OF THE IDEA OF MARKETING

Marketing, then, in the abstract, might be a vague and reified notion, but it connotes things that are universally agreed to be important, such as consumer sovereignty, competition and more efficient resource allocation, and the creation of jobs and wealth. The bringing of stuff to markets is not exactly new, but the technology, the goods, and the communication channels have changed, and the cultural presence of marketing as a management function and a metaphor for contemporary cultural life has grown out of sight. At the beginning of the boom in management studies in the 1960s Management guru Peter Drucker famously averred that marketing is one of just two value-adding activities in an organization, along with innovation. All the other activities, according to Drucker, are costs. Marketing's importance to organizations, from global multinationals to one-person businesses, can hardly be overstated, given that organizations of every type and size are defined by their engagement with markets. Whether this market-facing interchange has to be undertaken by one functional activity called "marketing" is quite another question. While its purpose and methods might be hard to pin down, the idea of marketing has spread like a virus. The scope of marketing as an organizational function once encompassed only the commercial sector, and focused mainly on products. Today, a marketing rationality based on service to all stakeholders, internal and external, has taken hold in much public, charitable and non-profit sector activity too. The ideology of the market holds sway in many government and local authority budgeting and sourcing decisions, and, in post-industrial Western economies, a marketing rationality governs not only consumer services but professional services like banking, law, medical treatment, and increasingly, education. Whether or not a marketing rationality in services and a marketing-inflected new public management mentality in government really improve performance and accountability, is an open question. Many would say not. Nonetheless, marketing in general has become a convenient label for practically all organizational value-adding activities, whether commercial, non-profit or charitable. Marketing really is the metaphor that just keeps on giving.

As a label for a very wide and varied collection of activities, marketing is supposed to serve organizations and their customers by revealing the all-important nuances in needs and wants and helping to fine-tune production and service to create a perfect match with consumer demand. This, at least, was the ethos of marketing when it emerged as a subject of study in German and then American universities at the turn of the twentieth century.[12] It was conceived as an economic and empirical discipline that took account of the heterogeneity of consumer demand. If this matching process is effective, then organizations and consumers are not the only ones to benefit. Society at large should benefit too, because consumers get the good stuff they want, and fewer resources are wasted on the bad stuff they don't. Marketing grows demand which creates opportunities for economies of scale, markets clear, profits are re-invested, competition drives innovation up and prices down, and the positive economic spiral widens.

Marketing also has a cultural heft beyond its roles as an organizational function and a social process of value exchange. The idea of marketing is so powerful it frequently obscures examinations of the particular detail of marketing. If the detail doesn't seem to add up, it's often rationalized as a failure of execution rather than a misunderstanding of the concept itself. In a neo-liberal age, the ideology of marketing strikes a resonant political note, since it captures and symbolizes freedom of choice and consumer sovereignty within a framework of competition in which big business must earn its power by personalizing its offers. Marketing has become a by-word for neo-liberal values of individualism, freedom under the law, competition and enterprise. Marketing is mooted as the bond between the individual consumer and big business, and it is conceived as the activity that delivers consumer sovereignty while giving the consumer more choice at lower cost. What's not to like?

Of course, there is much that is wrong with marketing, and there are countless examples where the bond of trust with the consumer has been based on falsehood and insincerity, with inevitable consequences for the public image of marketing. At the time of writing, in February 2013, the UK and Europe are embroiled in a scandal about the mislabeling of processed meat products. Some ready-meals described as containing beef have turned out to actually contain horsemeat and pork. This is being accounted for in the press as a supply chain fraud, but it will be seen as a marketing issue because, in the final analysis, it is the label which was misleading. But even though the *image* of marketing seems to plumb new depths with every successive consumer scandal, along with that of marketers, the *idea* of marketing as a managerial solution to the economic problems of the world seems to retain its rhetorical power. But the ideological force of the idea of marketing depends for much of its force on a gross oversimplification. Marketing is understood as *a* business function and *a* professional discipline, but there is an infinite diversity of practice that falls under that label. People do many very different things within marketing, sometimes spending an entire career within one sub-specialism such as personal selling, sales promotion, public relations, product development, direct mail, advertising, service management, design, logistics, buying, corporate communication, brand management, market research, strategy, pricing, merchandising, customer service operations, retail management, back office administration, tourism, or one of many more. The discipline of marketing management that is constituted through mass-selling text books is largely an oversimplified myth, while the idea of the market is another social construction that loses its notional unity under a close examination. There are, clearly, lots of different kinds of marketing, and lots of different kinds of market.

So, not only is marketing a label for a huge spectrum of professional activities in and around the stakeholders in and of organizations of every type, but it has also become a discourse, a way of talking about management, markets, and consumption. Many business terms have been parlayed into common usage by marketing textbooks, such as positioning, targeting, USP, market segmentation, customer service, consumer needs and wants, customer satisfaction, and the ubiquitous "market". It is easy to forget that, actually, the most successful practice is not based on the simplistic application of crude techniques or on the application of universal normative principles, but on precise attention to the detail of particular situations. Abstractions, acronyms and marketing jargon add the appearance of technical sophistication to marketing, but marketing is best conceived as a discipline that asks the right questions, and not as one that provides off-the-peg solutions.

## THE POLITICS OF MARKETING SCIENCE

Perhaps a more substantial sense of marketing could be found in the scientific aura that surrounds some of it. But, after more than a century as a university discipline, there is little or no applied scientific knowledge in marketing that managers would acknowledge. There is a lot of science and technology involved *in* marketing, in the form of, say, sophisticated "data mining" software, neuropsychological ("neuromarketing") research programs, internet algorithms that reveal my patterns of website viewing and parcel me up as a commodity to advertisers, copy-testing formulae that measure advertising response, and so on. There is even more science in academic marketing, with thousands of behavioral and cognitive experiments that test the responses of small, unrepresentative samples of consumers to particular sets of marketing stimuli. Yet, despite all this effort, marketing's connection with the everyday experience of consumers and practitioners often remains aphoristic and anecdotal. There are no general principles of application that stand up to a robust examination, and there is no widely agreed body of knowledge beyond the standard textbook axioms that newly minted managers abandon in their first week of real work. There is much science *in* marketing, but no scientific principles *of* marketing. There is an academic marketing enterprise that searches for empirical generalizations about markets and consumption, but these are so elusive and, if found, esoteric, that they do not easily assist practitioners. For academics, the pursuit of research, rather than the generation of answers, is essential to hone skills of scholarship, to engage with other social and human disciplines, and to raise the curriculum beyond anecdote and cliché. For practical people in marketing, though, business academics have no easy solutions to offer, for all our vaunted research.

Further complicating the pursuit of science in the cause of marketing knowledge is the political role marketing research assumes within organizations, as a device of communication and consensus building for internal budget and strategy decisions. A great deal of highly successful marketing practice is based on informed judgment, intuition, and experiential knowledge, not to mention chance and chutzpah, but everyone's intuition is different and it is much easier to win consensus on major budget decisions if there are some scientific-looking correlations to throw up on the bar chart at the board meeting. This political aspect of organizational life is important. There is politics in every field, in the sense that people in organizations have to negotiate alliances of mutual self-interest if they want to get things done. Management, especially, is a deeply political function in organizations, since it is predicated on claiming, and wielding, power and authority. Ask any marketing manager who has ever tried to get changes in product design or price agreed by the main board, or who has tried to argue for an increase in marketing budget during a recession. If this political aspect of marketing management is forgotten, it can mean that marketing action is rationalized in terms of the formal research and strategy. Informal organizational processes, including the politics and the implicit dimensions[13] of marketing practice, can be sidelined. The discourse of science plays a big part in the organizational power game, since evidence from the market must often be presented as if it is scientific in order to gain agreement on strategic decisions. Science is not only invoked in advertisements that use white-coated, grey haired, male, actors to sell washing powder as if they are Einsteins of detergent.[14] It is also invoked internally in marketing organizations as part of the power politics of strategy.

As an organizational function, marketing operates within a context of organizational politics populated by other competing disciplines. In many cases, in my experience of talking to practitioners, marketing is by no means the most respected or politically the most powerful functional discipline. Marketing may be acknowledged as the function that delivers the bottom line, but this isn't always matched by a sense of respect for either the power of its methods, or the skills of its practitioners. As a result the idea of the marketing manager as a conduit linking consumer insight with product development, pricing policy and the rest falls apart. Most marketing professionals lack the organizational power to fulfill their function in the way the textbooks describe. Production, design, and operations often hold sway over product decisions, finance over pricing, operations and supply chain over distribution. The marketing person often works in a silo, lacking the budget or authority to control the outcomes by which they are judged. Perhaps this paints a bleak picture of the marketing role, and no doubt there are countless notable exceptions. But it is equally true that many graduates of MBAs and marketing programmes are dismayed at the huge gap they find between the hyperbolic way the marketing management role is described in their textbooks and classes, and the way it plays out in the cold reality of organizational politics. I think improved credibility for the discipline rests partly in a more grounded contextual approach that can be communicated with nuance and detail.

The political role of science can be particularly tense in advertising. Statistical testing is imposed on most creative executions (the ad) before campaign launch. Mock-ups or animations of ads are shown via the internet (called "link tests") to a group of consumers who volunteer to be paid participants. Their responses are checked against predetermined formulae, and if they don't match up with suitably high likeability scores, the ad is canned and the agency account team is sent back to the drawing board. This is usually met with fury from creative teams who regard advertising research in general, and advertising "copy testing" in particular as anathema to the creativity and risk-taking that underpins great advertising. For the creative professionals who make the ads, subjecting advertising to pseudo-scientific tests caricatures the way real consumers engage with advertising. This pseudo-science, though, is necessary for clients who need it to justify budgets to their board. For decades, advertising has been conceived by researchers in the business as if it was a mediated personal sales encounter. This mistaken analogy still blights much of the advertising business.[15]

The chimera of marketing science, though, retains its force. As I write, global FMCG multinationals are hiring teams of neuroscientists to run their MRI (magnetic resonance imaging) scanning machines so they can test brain responses to marketing stimuli. I'm reliably informed that many of these organizations won't allow so much as a strapline out of the door before it's subjected to neuro-testing. Since Vance Packard's famous exposé of advertising's use of depth psychology to reveal consumers' hidden motivations,[16] marketing has had a public image as a dark, subterranean world of sophisticated, quasi-scientific manipulation. In fact, marketing can be as naive as the most credulous consumer when it comes to taking on board the latest sciency fad for consumer control. Don't get me wrong, there's a lot of clever stuff going on. But a science of consumer control in marketing is still a very long way off. Marketing neuroscience is probably the biggest distraction in marketing since phrenologists were routinely hired for their consumer behavioral insights.[17]

## SUMMARY: CONTEXTUAL MARKETING AND COMPETING KNOWLEDGE

Marketing, then, may not be an emperor without clothes but it certainly lacks an overcoat. The fact that its garments are so threadbare makes its enigmatic presence as a cultural idea, an academic research program and a business ideology, all the more fascinating. Marketing in organizations operates in a wider context not only of consumer culture but of other organizational functions. In connection with its internal organizational role, marketing intersects with exterior fields of knowledge and practice. Claims about marketing are made and received within the context of other knowledge, and marketing insights that may seem a matter of common sense to practitioners working day-to-day at the customer interface, often face a difficult task of communication in order to sell their insights to main board members or other senior internal stakeholders. This is where market and consumer research assumes an acutely political role in organizations, rhetorically justifying management decisions. I've alluded above to my skepticism about the quality of insights yielded by neuropsychological research in marketing, but I have no doubt of its great political weight. The source credibility of a white-coated doctor in detergent advertising has long been well known. When someone with the word "neuro" in their job title points to a graph and tells the main board that a logo works well on a sample of brains, it would take a pretty confident and fairly reckless marketing officer to contradict that. Many of the most exciting marketing initiatives, though, have been matters of intuition that were counter-intuitive to everyone else. There was no science, and sometimes no consensus. In most organizations, creative ideas have to percolate through a defensive and risk-averse rationality. I see the contextual approach to marketing as a way of helping to make consumer insight more transparent, not in a technically obtuse way but in a way which spans competing organizational knowledge.

Marketing practice, then, may be most usefully thought of as a program of informed inquiry rather than a set of normative precepts. It has plenty of science, but none that can tell you how to *do* marketing in a given context. Indeed, much of its science conceives the experience of marketing in terms of a laboratory test, and the consumer of marketing as a robot. In other words, it fails to take account of the most important aspect of marketing: the consumer cultural context.

So, researchers have been looking for marketing's scientific hot button for quite some time, but we've been looking in the wrong place. And the worse news is that it isn't so much a hot button as a warm blancmange. This book, then, draws on the logic of advertising and brand planning to set out a view of marketing as a process embedded in cultural context. In other words, everything in marketing is contingent. There are no boil-in-the-bag solutions. Nonetheless, I hope in this book to demystify marketing as an informed mode of commercially inflected social inquiry, rather than complicate it as an enigmatic science. I will go beyond the commonplace claim that environment influences behavior, to argue that marketing effects can only be properly understood by considering them within a dynamic and relational consumer cultural context. The mise-en-scéne analogy hints at the aesthetic and emotional character of audience activation in marketing. It also points to the role of the marketing professional, not in controlling environmental stimuli, but in setting the scene to best effect in order to elicit the engagement and activate the emotions of the audience of marketing, the consumer. My intention overall in the book is not to generate a new theory, but to try to reflect the pragmatic, fluid, and nuanced way that marketing is understood by top advertising and branding account planners. I feel that typical business school theory routinely adopts a piecemeal and reductionist cause-effect approach, and I argue that an appreciation of consumer cultural context, the marketing scene, offers an altogether richer account of marketing influence.

# CHAPTER 2

# Marketing as Communication

## *OREO* AND SUPERBOWL 2013

I want to continue exploring the image of the consumer as a member of the audience at a performance, with another brief example of almost-but-not-quite, off-the-cuff marketing. Like the Dr Dre example in Chapter 1, this one can be seen, on the face of it, as merely a minor piece of promotional flair, perhaps the digital equivalent of P.T. Barnum blustering about his latest exhibit, or "Colonel" Tom Parker selling signed photos of Elvis at the stage door while the main man wowed the crowd in Las Vegas. The arch marketing chutzpah of both these iconic hard-sellers was unorthodox, but I think it would be wrong to dismiss them as purveyors of petty promotional wheezes on the periphery of *real* marketing. Likewise, the efficacy of Dr Dre's intrusion into Olympic swimming and Oeros' exploitation of a dud plug at the Superdome were probably over-hyped in the marketing trade press, but it would be similarly mistaken to dismiss them as outliers to the real story of marketing management analysis, planning and control. In fact, I'd argue that the role of communication in marketing has been consistently played down in the managerial marketing textbooks in favour of a much simpler, and less accurate, mechanistic model of the marketing process. After all, what is a market but a forum of communication? The interesting thing about both the Dr Dre and the Oreos examples is that picking them apart reveals layers of context without which neither initiative would be any richer in significance than a product flyer blown down the street off the side of a bus shelter. The fact of creating a communication meant nothing without the context, and the understanding of the context gave meaning to the communication.

I drew out the contextual description of Dr Dre's product placement in the previous chapter to underline the idea that abstract categories such as product placement, or ambush marketing, tell us little about the dynamics of a situation unless we also have a full understanding of the whole context. Another piece of mischievous marketing opportunism that received a lot of media coverage occurred during the American Superbowl of January 2013. The now notorious power outage that plunged the *Mercedes Benz Superdome* into semi-darkness and halted the game between the Baltimore Ravens and the San Francisco 49ers for half an hour had advertisers in a sweat in case some of the reported 108 million viewers might lose interest and drift away from their TV sets. The Superbowl provides an advertising platform with a potential reach of no less than one in two American households. Some viewers naturally resorted to their phones to pass the time when play was stopped and checked their Twitter feed. Amongst the many lame blackout joke-promotions was a sharper one that biscuit brand Oreos Tweeted within minutes of the lights fading. The headline exclaimed "Power Out? No problem" over a picture of the biscuit with the strapline "You can still dunk in the dark." Two days later, the ad had been re-Tweeted over 14,000 times according to reports. In addition, it generated thousands of admiring column inches of comment in the media and marketing press[1] and many more thousands of "likes" on Facebook pages devoted to the brand. Oreos were not the only brand trying to piggy back on the blackout with social media quips, but by general consent they were the only brand that actually pulled it off.

The ad might have been made up on the hoof in response to an unpredictable event, but it was, nonetheless, a planned piece of opportunism. *Time* magazine[2] reported that Oreo's advertising agency *360i* claimed to have been waiting for an opportunity for some spontaneous Superbowl promotion.

The full marketing team and ad agency staff were assembled, watching the game and ready to pounce on any watercooler moment that occurred during play. When half the floodlights in the stadium dimmed making play impossible, the Oreos team were able to quickly get their brainstorm into production and have approval signed off without the usual layers of bureaucracy and creativity-killing copy-testing. This has been called newsjacking, the art of trying to tie a promotion into a topical news item. But the principles of spontaneity, creativity and wit can be applied in any marketing context. Practitioners who spend all their time waiting for a news item to hijack could spend an awful lot of time watching TV and social media. That's my job. Oreos had calculated that there was a high probability of an incident that they could exploit arising during the four hours or more of Superbowl, so the principle they were applying was to be creative and spontaneous in a specifically calculated context. It wasn't about newsjacking; it was about the application of creativity in context.

The cheeky Oreo Tweet leveraged the spot advertising the brand had already bought during the game, and, of course, chimed with the fans who had a supply of Oreos to hand to dunk in their coffee or milk (or beer) as part of their in-game grazing strategy. With the team assembled ready to spot real-time social media marketing opportunities, the power failure was an object lesson in opportunity falling to those who are ready to take it. If the account is to be believed, they probably had some other scenarios mapped out before the blackout gave them that unexpected creative opportunity. The re-Tweets, Facebook likes and trade media coverage reflected the goodwill with which the ad was received, and provided a welcome moment of light relief (pun intended) for fans from the frustrating hiatus in the game. Superbowl sells the most expensive spot advertising in TV, about $3.8 million for a 30-second slot at the 2013 game, according to the *Wall Street Journal*.[3] Tweets are free, but PR is priceless. Most Superbowl ads assume that their outlay will generate some PR coverage, simply because there is such a buzz around Superbowl ads every year, but the Oreo initiative won the prize this year for the most-talked-about ad, in a year which by common consent was not a vintage one for Superbowl ads.

## SOCIAL MEDIA AND MASS AUDIENCE PLATFORMS

Some would doubt the advantages that a Twitter-buzz can confer on a brand. After all, as everyone knows, vivid advertising that is endlessly repeated can browbeat the unreflexive consumer into autonomic acquiescence. Why does it help a brand to provide social media entertainment for consumers who might not even be buyers? John B. Watson, the acade mic-psychologist-turned-advertising-man with JWT, became famous for applying his theories of behaviorism to the selling game. He treated consumers as if they were indeed automatons who learned through behavioral conditioning, and it seemed to work. Repetition and reinforcement sells, for lowest-common-denominator brands with deep pockets, at least. Campaigns for *Radion* detergent in the 1990s come to mind, and more recent ones for *McDonald*'s or *Cillit Bang*. These are just horrible ads that demand to be heard, like the loudest child at the party. To be fair, even the brand monoliths like *McDonald*'s who use ubiquitous presence as a strategy, do know how to connect with their audience with creativity from time to time, and they certainly understand the cultural milieu of their key markets. Detergent ads have a stridency that has become so familiar, the genre has turned into self-parody, and *Cillit Bang* ads wallow in it (they have to be self-parody – don't they?) *McDonald*'s, on the other hand, sometimes uses slice-of-life stories that say "we understand you," but the arches and the deeply sinister clown are seldom far from shot. I say this only partly because some very nice ad agency creatives working on the *McDonald*'s account kindly granted me an interview. But, notwithstanding some neat variations on the theme, in general, high-presence, high volume, mass media advertising doesn't try to be too clever because it doesn't need to. It just shifts product by forcing the brand into the public consciousness, like a cultural suppository.

But advertising doesn't just do one thing, and it doesn't only work in one way. Since Ernest Dichter's motivational research in the 1960s,[4] it has been evident that the advertising audience is not purely passive. The best ads succeed by being talked about, and social media is a word of mouth (WOM) multiplier. Stories about brands are told and retold, and they feed into the brand mythology, extending its meaning and its cultural reach. The logic of brand equity is that the more the brand is talked about, the greater the effect should be on market share in the long term. Cultural presence alone isn't enough – there must be stories that connect with the audience. There is, still, a need for mass advertising – it can't be beaten for getting a story into living rooms, bars, and Twitter feeds, and for generating chat around company water coolers, almost instantly. It is much harder than it once was, though, to find media platforms that deliver big numbers of affluent viewers in real time. Media audiences have fragmented and media vehicles have multiplied. The Superbowl retains its prestige as a TV advertising platform because of the way audiences are falling away from other mass media vehicles. Real time TV viewing figures of 20 million are now exceptional in the USA,[5] while in the UK the top shows most weeks boast 10 or 11 million. Some 30 years ago, a UK TV entertainment show would have to reach an audience 30 million to challenge for the top spot. Today, big sports events, covered live on TV, are the last major real-time mass audience platforms. Platform, though, is no longer quite the right metaphor because the way mass media advertising is used is changing. It is being seen less as a piece of TV drama viewed passively by the audience, and more as an opportunity to create an engagement that activates the consumer. Indeed, the activation part is so important that social media supporting mass media campaigns are not merely the virtual front of house staff engaging directly with the audience – they can sometimes be more important than the mass advertising main show. Promotional channel boundaries are bleeding into each other and the interstices between them often yield some of the richest, and most cost effective, examples of clever contextual marketing communication.

I make no claim about the sales effectiveness of either the Dr Dre or *Oreo*'s examples. I do maintain there are wider lessons for marketers. Platform events viewed in real time by mass audiences afford special opportunities for spontaneous and creative marketing through social media. The *360i* team understood that media consumption has changed. Many people today engage interactively with social media by receiving and sending mobile messages whilst they are watching TV. Indeed, some people engage in social media on mobile devices whilst they are sitting in my lectures, a development in media consumption I still haven't quite got used to. As audiences splinter across ever-increasing numbers of media channels and media vehicles, these mass audience events deserve special attention from marketers, and maybe even a little paid overtime for the marketing team putting in those additional weekend hours on Twitter.

Social media marketing offers opportunities to leverage mass media coverage to elicit consumer activation, in addition to generating presence for the brand. There are still opportunities for presence. Sports sponsorship or sports event advertising is the area that can, still, yield presence aplenty, but passive marketing is now regarded as old hat. Presence without activation is seen as an opportunity missed. This can be done physically, by manning experiential events within the sponsored event to engage face-to-face with people, or it can be done virtually, through social media. Social media marketing makes it so much easier for brands to leverage presence they paid for in other media, just as the Oreo's Tweet leveraged their paid-for Superbowl ads.

## SOCIAL MEDIA, RESEARCH, AND CONSUMER INSIGHT

To be fair, my two examples of what I would describe as forms of cultural placement, fall under the banner of communication and don't encompass the entire scope of marketing activity. Nonetheless, they are instructive on several levels. Most strikingly, they exemplify the closeness to the consumer that can be facilitated by mass media in concert with social media. It is a cliché to say that marketing communication is now a conversation in contrast to the old, analogue, loud hailer model of marketing communication, but it bears closer examination. The epiphanies to consumer "orientation" so beloved of marketing text books usually have little to say about how that might be achieved, other than through something called "research" feeding into strategy. Research, though, can be a very blunt instrument. Social media conversations offer a more fluid way of understanding the idiom of consumer markets. Indeed, engaging in social media conversations with consumers is a form of research, in an informal, literary sense. It can also be seen as a form of quasi-ethnography.[6]

Formal research in marketing organizations can, at worst, become a self-serving exercise designed to generate post-hoc justification for decisions already made. For example, according to quite a few marketing textbooks, "research" seems principally to mean one thing: the questionnaire survey. Questionnaire surveys can have their uses in some situations, but they are very difficult indeed to get right. Using them as the default research method rarely plays to their strength. Like its equivalent in the brutal world of state oppression, the forced confession, the questionnaire survey coerces the participant to offer views on matters into which they may have little or no insight, but without the sleep deprivation. Surveys typically suffer from devastating sampling and non-response problems, and even if they are sincerely filled in by a person in the intended sample frame, they cannot get around the problem of self-reporting. When asked about our behavior or attitudes, we simply don't know most of the answers. There is no semantic scale yet devised that allows a response of "I can't really remember" or "well, it depends." There really are only two ways to understand consumers. One is spending time with them, talking to them, watching them, and learning how they see the world. The other is to use methods that allow consumers to articulate or demonstrate aspects of their experience in a way that is immediate and accessible. Data gathering methods that strip the context out of human action invariably miss crucial detail, and we often don't have much insight into our own behavior and motivations until we get the opportunity to reflect on them in a congenial space. Social media can be a proxy for consumer ethnography, the anthropological approach of understanding a culture by becoming part of it, because they provide virtual access to an often unguarded engagement with quite intimate aspects of consumer experience. There is the added advantage, at times like Superbowl evening, to tap into this consciousness in real time, at exactly the time consumers are experiencing the event. Overall, formal research in marketing can be useful if carefully designed but it is often used simplistically or naively. Social media have opened up ways of accessing consumer insights more effectively, cheaply, and quickly.

Granted, watching the Superbowl at the same time as consumers, and simultaneously exchanging social media messages with them, might not constitute a chapter in most business research methods textbooks, but it is an obvious form of parallel ethnography. The questionnaire survey asks a person about their life using terms and values they may not recognize. It also asks people to reconstitute facts or memories they may not accurately recall. Quasi-ethnographic methods, for example, indulging in the same entertainment as the target audience and exchanging real time social media messages with them, might seem flaky and subjective to some researchers who are of a natural scientific disposition. As a research method, virtual ethnography lacks precision, and it rests on subjective interpretation. But watching and engaging with consumers through social media can achieve a greater integrity of insight than more formal, arms-length methods because of its ecological validity and its contextual integrity. Social media offer an open window into consumer cultures. There is no need to set up artificial situations in laboratories in order to elicit measurable responses. Formal research methods often sacrifice ecological validity for methodological neatness. Don't give me a questionnaire asking me what TV channel I viewed last week – I can take a running guess but I can't really remember whether I watched a particular show last week or last year. Through social media you can see what I'm watching right now if I'm talking about it on Twitter.

## CONSUMER INSIGHT AND CULTURAL TRANSLATION

Loathe as they might be to admit it, business executives don't necessarily occupy the same social milieu as their key market segments. Understanding consumers is not merely a matter of collating the data. The resulting insight depends on the integrity of cultural translation, which in turn depends on how those data are interpreted. Philosophers have a term they call indexicality, meaning the referent to which language points. If you overhear a conversation, you might take a guess at what the people are talking about, but you might get it completely wrong. Conversation often misses out on stating what is implicitly understood between the speakers. Repairing indexicality means using an understanding of the social context that frames a conversation to understand what a passage of text spoken or written by someone means. You might not fully understand a reported conversation if you weren't there, and you're unlikely to fully understand the indexicality of a qualitative, talk-based data set unless you understand the idiom that makes the conversation meaningful. Given that marketing practitioners cannot reasonably be expected to become part of all the social groups they serve, generating consumer insight demands an order of translation that is far more than a mechanistic matter of collating data sets and counting categories. Social media may allow a degree of access to context, but cultural translation is needed to convey the contextualized meaning of the data. In other words, you can never avoid the necessity of interpretation.

The simplest route to closeness to the consumer is to walk in the consumers' shoes, in much the same way as the anthropologist tries to do to understand cultures. Marketing in general can be understood as a form of cultural ethnography in the sense that it has the task of generating insight into the cultural milieu of consumers, and then translating this insight into something that can be infused into marketing strategies. Arguably, though, the area of consumer insight has been neglected in marketing management approaches that emphasize abstract process categories or arthritic research methods, and ignore the role of cultural translation in generating actionable and nuanced consumer insight. Social media constitute a public communication space that is conducted in a private conversational idiom, a fact of which I tell my children to be more aware in case a future employer doesn't share their friends' Facebook humor (they ignore me). As a result of the merging of private/public in social media, social media offer invaluable research tools for contextual marketing, not just for crowd sourcing ideas, which can prove un-manageable, but for generating insight into the way meaning is formed within a social milieu. Research seldom speaks for itself, but if marketing professionals occupy the same social milieu as consumers, even for a short time and in a mediated, virtual form, it doesn't necessarily have to.

## CONSUMER INSIGHT AND *DOVE CFRB* SOCIAL MARKETING[7]

A somewhat more formal approach to consumer insight was claimed as the basis for the controversial *Dove "Campaign for Real Beauty"* (CfRB) that, reportedly, raised the brand's UK market share by 30% in a couple of years. This much-commented-upon social marketing campaign was partly based on the use of social media and began in 2003. It exploited the backlash in some Western countries against the photo-shopped artificiality of conventional cosmetic advertising. Social marketing is a subset of marketing in which good causes or ethical aims form a part of the appeal. So, for example, a government advertising campaign to promote safer driving or to encourage healthier eating might fall under the label social marketing. Quite a number of commercial brands see the advantages in this and have adopted a social marketing positioning by linking with an ethical cause. From a marketing perspective, this can be understood as an astute way to create an emotional connection with consumers who identify strongly with that same cause. The link might be made tangible by, for example, donating a proportion of revenue to a charitable foundation, or, better still, starting a charitable foundation in the name of the brand.

The *Dove* campaign was premised on an issue that was topical in the UK at the time. The use of photo-shopped images of very thin models in fashion and cosmetics advertising had come into disrepute in some quarters as a putative cause of low self-esteem among women, and possibly even as a factor in eating disorders such as anorexia. The key consumer insight for *Dove*'s repositioning was that conventional, aspirational ("*Revlon* don't sell cosmetics, we sell hope"[8]) cosmetics advertising played on women's low self-esteem by making them feel insecure about their appearance. It hardly seems necessary to add that advertisements featuring sexualized (i.e., semi-nude and attractive) images of men are becoming far more common in the wake of decades of sexualization of women in advertising. What is more, many more men, apparently, are engaging in the cosmetic surgery market as a result of feeling that their bodies aren't quite up to scratch. Traditional cosmetics and fashion branding present ideals of beauty that are unattainable, even for the models themselves, since every asymmetry and blemish is photo-shopped away. The team had garnered from interviews that a large group of women resented conventional cosmetics advertising because it didn't represent real women. They just didn't think this style of advertising was relevant to them. The team wanted to feed this insight into a counter-revolutionary campaign featuring "real" (i.e., not photo-shopped or size zero) women. As the story goes, the predominantly male, middle aged *Unilever* board resisted this radical move until presented with videos of their own wives and daughters explaining how insecure typical cosmetics ads made them feel about their bodies. The idea was sold and *Dove CfRB* was born.

*Dove* positioned their brand as giving (or to be accurate, selling) women's self-esteem back to them. The theme was expanded across different media platforms with clever PR and initiatives including the *Dove* self-esteem website,[9] charitable donations to *Dove*'s Self-Esteem Fund, and some striking viral videos, including one called "Evolution" of a model being photoshopped, made by Ogilvy Toronto[10] (and a follow up called "Onslaught" focusing on the influence advertising might exert on young girls' self-image). The positioning was controversial, at least for cynics who pointed out that Unilever also operate a stable of brands that hardly demur from exploiting beauty stereotypes. Unilever's men's deodorant brands *Lynx* and *Axe* are notorious for their ads sexualizing women, while the skin whitener *Fair & Lovely* exploits Western beauty myths about light skin in the African subcontinent and South, as well as South East, Asia. What is more, *Dove*'s social marketing strategy seems to have been eschewed altogether in international markets that don't buy into the media criticism of aspirational, sexualized and fantasy-based cosmetics marketing, such as Hong Kong.[11]

The interesting thing (to me) was that the *Dove CfRB* campaign was apparently based on an insight that would probably have eluded conventional marketing research. It required an appreciation of the wider context of the issue (beauty myths and the visual representation of women in media) including the way this topic was playing out as a media debate in Western fashion circles. This issue was expanded by *Dove* to take in wider cultural issues of female children's psychological development and women's education and social role. This seems to be an example of consumer insight that was generated by sensitively using qualitative interviews in a way that was flexible enough to accommodate contextual insights from consumer culture. These insights would have fallen well outside the usual remit of more structured marketing research methods. The result radically challenged the Western discourse of cosmetics advertising. I say challenged the "discourse" rather than the values, because all that is challenged is the form of representation. *Dove*'s 2013 viral campaign called "Thought Before Action" (see it on YouTube[12]) offered a piece of software that secretly reverted photographs to their un-photoshopped state. A number of commentators pointed to the contradictions of this approach. An acerbic blog from a brand consultancy called Quo Vadis[13] pointed out that, while female body image is unquestionably manipulated by marketers, *Dove* is not exactly above the fray with its enhanced photography of the products (a bar of used soap never really looked this good), its chemical masking of the way the products really look and smell, and its alleged double-standard in exploiting ideologies of female beauty by claiming to take a stand against them. Leaving aside ongoing debate about the ethical integrity of *Dove CfRB*, one can hardly doubt its success in using a relatively informal research-based insight to engage powerfully with an important group of consumers.

I will return to the theme of marketing research and context later in the book. For now I want to expand a little more on the reasons why I identify communication as such a fruitful source of insight into marketing.

## SOCIAL MEDIA BITES BACK – THE *FEMFRESH* LAUNCH LEAVES A BAD TASTE

The immediacy and spontaneity of social media rewards a cultivated sensitivity to context, while it punishes a lack of contextual understanding. Feminine hygiene brand *FemFresh* rolled out ads for its new product with much fanfare in 2012 and added a Facebook page that tried to engage users with synonyms for vagina, including (ahem) froo froo, va jay jay, kitty[14] and many more you'd be familiar with if you've seen Eve Ensler's *Vagina Monologues*. The Facebook page was quickly overrun with complaints on two grounds. One was the view that the product was being sold as an essential as opposed to an optional accessory to femininity, and therefore it targeted the body insecurity of (particularly young) women. The other was that many women would prefer a more candid and less patronizing use of the proper term. The brand might have assumed that women would engage in a collective laugh of relief that some of the cruder synonyms for vagina (such as a "Jeremy Clarkson") had been avoided. But they were wrong. The Facebook campaign imploded with some force which begged the question of how a major brand could possibly have managed to tap so surely into this virulent strain of consumer antipathy.

Truth is, there is always a risk in social media marketing, just as there is in any creative marketing initiative. Anyone can get it wrong from time to time. My point in relating this hoo hah over the hoo hoo is that a thorough understanding of the full social context surrounding this product and its consumers might well have forewarned the brand about the risks of this particular creative execution. The example also raises another topic that is central to a contextual under-standing of marketing. That is, language is far from being a neutral medium for the conveyance of a message. Rather, language is a constitutive element of meaning. Linguistic idiom is one of the key currencies of marketing, as anyone will attest who remembers Whasaaaaap, Got Milk? Because You're Worth It, Just Do It, Vorsprung Durch Technik and countless other irritatingly memorable marketing tag lines. The *FemFresh* Froo Froo brouhaha created a powerful audience connection – unfortunately, it opened a channel for dissent, which was freely and candidly expressed. Our friend indexicality is relevant again here. A full understanding of the cultural context into which this copywriting firecracker was dropped might just have enabled the agency to repair the indexicality and grasp the meanings that were likely to be construed by the target audience.

There may have been an element of bad luck involved, to be fair to the *FemFresh* marketing team. Just days before the *FemFresh* launch had created such a fuss it was widely reported[15] that the use of the V-word had left a bad taste in the mouths of Michigan politicians. They had censured Democrat Lisa Brown for calling a vagina a vagina during a tetchy debate on abortion in the Michigan House of representatives. The use of the word was deemed offensive by male politicians. The press coverage this received may have inflamed sensibilities just in time for *FemFresh* to blunder in and present an opportunity to women already angered by what they saw as the patronizing prissy-ness of some, male, Michigan Senators. The idea probably seemed like a bit of slightly edgy but ultimately harmless fun to the brand team. Nonetheless, the suspicion remains that this most difficult of creative briefs might have been more successfully executed with a stronger appreciation of the consumer cultural context in which the campaign would be received.

## *BODYFORM* MAKES FUN OF ITS OWN PERIOD MYTH

Continuing the theme of marketing targeted at women, the *Bodyform* brand's social media exchange with a man who claimed to have believed their advertising, earned a better reception. A Facebook post attributed to aspiring author "Richard"[16] (who wanted to plug his book) lamented that watching *Bodyform* advertising over the years led him to believe that, once a month, his female friends would be the most terrific fun, taking him bike riding, skiing, mountain climbing or horseriding and enjoying life with a verve he would hardly be able to match. The reality, he claimed, was sadly different, reminding him more of a scene from the movie *The Exorcist*, in which the main female character gets a little tetchy, and he blamed the advertising for creating this altogether misleading impression. The post went viral and earned 40,000 likes in a day. Just four days later, *Bodyform* had a witty video response on YouTube with an actress in the role of *Bodyform* CEO explaining the true nature of periods to Richard. When I last checked, the video had earned over 3.7 million views.[17] SCR, manufacturers of *Bodyform*, and their ad agency Carat, picked up on Richard's Facebook joke and ran with it, supported by astute PR. Much admiring press comment followed, adding to the buzz.[18]

As with the *Oreos* example, this PR gold strike was very much a team effort that derived from a rapid and co-ordinated creative response to an event that chimed with the target audience. An example of newsjacking perhaps, but once again, the context was everything. The sensitivity of the subject did not mean that humor and self-parody were regarded as too risky – in fact, the self-deprecating act in the *Bodyform* video struck exactly the right note. The value for money of this exposure in comparison to a paid-for TV spot is palpable. Getting almost 4 million views of a 1 minute 45 seconds TV ad could take several million in production, even before the TV spots were paid for. A video for YouTube normally costs tens of thousands, or less. Consider that viewers actively sought out the video to watch it and share it with friends, as opposed to half-listening to it during a TV ad break, and you have the essence of branded content: active consumer engagement. The script writing was astute – the YouTube video parodied sanitary pad promotion, but it also invoked *Bodyform*'s tradition of advertising in an admiring way that dovetailed nicely with the brand history. The tone of this social media exchange was, perhaps, rather British – the humor of the video seemed offbeat and a little weird or vulgar to some. This unique marketing initiative was founded on an acute sensitivity to the particular context in which the exchange would be received. The brand took a piece of ad hoc social media engagement and leveraged it to magnify the effect – from 40,000 Facebook likes to 3.7 million YouTube views, plus thousands of words of admiring media editorial, to boot.

## COMMUNICATION RECEPTION IN MARKETING

These examples may be of a type but they do illustrate the limitations of naive, linear models of marketing communication.[19] To be sure, lowest-common-denominator, join-the-dots marketing appeals that alert the consumer's conscious Attention, elicit their Interest, provoke their Desire and eventually motivate them to Action when they buy the product or service (A-I-D-A, for short) can, no doubt, lead some sheep into the pen. But the examples above bring home the way some of the most astute marketing plays with the open semiotic space of public communication. Just as the mise-en-scéne leaves the viewer to complete the hermeneutic circle and derive meaning from the scene, the most interesting marketing communication engages in a knowing conversation with the audience. What it doesn't do is to try to reduce the complexity and nuance of human communication to a hegemonic, univocal message that will not generate resistance or dissent. The polysemic potential of advertising and marketing communication, the possibilities for the message to be read in many different ways, is something clever marketing communication embraces. Less clever marketing communication tries to crush the polysemic potential of promotional communication by mechanizing creativity. Loud hailer models like AIDA don't map on to a social media environment which the brand cannot hope to control. Instead, brands have to try to participate sensitively in the conversation.

There is a vast literature in marketing and consumer research showing the ways consumers use, interpret, re-interpret, resist and co-create marketing communication, but you'd be hard pressed to see much of it cited in the mass-selling text books. The 100-year-old Attention–Interest–Desire–Action sequence, which was devised to model the psychology of personal selling[20] and later applied to mass advertising, is a staple of marketing text books. It is still used in some ad agencies too, but it caricatures the mediated communication process, and rests on some very dubious assumptions. These dubious assumptions include:

1. The consumer is persuaded by rational, utility-based appeals.
2. The meaning of marketing messages is univocal and controllable.
3. Marketing persuasion operates on a conscious rather than unconscious level.
4. Mass media communication is analogous to a personal sales conversation.

These four principles are often used as working assumptions for campaign strategy, but none of them stands up well to careful analysis. Human communication is more complex than this.

Take an example from political advertising. The most famous political advertising poster in British history, and one of the most lauded British posters of any kind, was produced by Saatchi and Saatchi for the Conservative Party's 1980 election bid. The poster featured a queue of people, snaking from a sign saying "Employment Office." On the top in huge capital letters were the words "LABOUR ISN'T WORKING." In the bottom right corner, in smaller letters, were added the words "Britain's better off with the Conservatives." The reader is left to infer the intended meaning by drawing on his or her cultural knowledge. In order to "get" the ad, the reader has to understand the pun on "working," which refers both to a general failure of Labour party policies, and a literal lengthening of queues of unemployed people outside employment offices. The reader would need to know that people queued up in employment offices to see the clerk, and they would have to infer that Labour Party policies had caused the queue to lengthen. In fact, the poster apparently failed to elicit much voter attention until the Labour Party discovered that the people photographed in the poster were not in fact unemployed, but were Conservative party activists. This deceit (these were innocent days in British political advertising) was mentioned by Labour in the House of Parliament with the intention of discrediting the Conservatives. The ploy backfired, the poster became famous and was credited with winning the 1980 election for the Conservatives[21] and Margaret Thatcher.

Granted, Labour Isn't Working was not selling a product. Nonetheless, in this and many other examples throughout this book, I hope the point is made that marketing has an open-textured aspect that relies intimately on forms of mutual understanding that are tacit, rather than explicit, and which draw on shared knowledge of the consumer cultural context. Consumers can be seen as an audience in a theatre, and their interpretation of the scene takes in the entire context, including, in this case, events happening off stage. Incidentally, unemployment continued to rise under the Conservative government.

## EDWARD BERNAYS AND THE SOCIAL SCIENCE OF PUBLIC RELATIONS

If AIDA still strikes you as a realistic way to conceive of marketing communication, consider the extraordinary story of Edward Bernays and his "torches of freedom." Bernays, Sigmund Freud's nephew, applied the nascent ideas of psychoanalysis and crowd psychology to the business of propaganda. He helped popularize the idea of democracy during the Second World War, but his personal view was that the masses needed to be led, rather than consulted. Bernays felt that a consumer society should rightly involve the manipulation of public opinion by corporations, to keep the masses amused and distracted, for their good and the good of an ordered and stable society. He saw the discipline of influencing public opinion through news media as a social science of benign manipulation. After the war, Bernays set up a press agency in New York and invented the term Public Relations, since he felt that "propaganda" was too loaded with wartime connotations. Hence, Public Relations itself is a public relations initiative.

Charged with a brief to persuade more American women to take up cigarette smoking, Bernays realized that he had to undermine the severe social stigma that surrounded female smoking at that time. Women could even be arrested for public smoking. He commissioned a psychoanalyst (not his uncle) to explain that cigarettes were symbolic penises, and if women were persuaded to smoke, they would have their own penises, and with them, a sense of male power. Bernays saw an opportunity at the New York Easter Parade of 1929, which he knew would be heavily covered by press and TV reporters. He hired a group of debutantes to join the parade. At a given signal, they would take out *Lucky Strike* cigarettes from their garters, and light up. This shocking sight was sure to attract the attention of the camera crews and journalists. Bernays told the women to say they were demanding their rights by lighting up "torches of freedom." He thought this term would evince an emotional response because of the metaphoric visual link with the Statue of Liberty. The newsreels duly presented the sight of smoking debutantes as a spontaneous protest on behalf of women's self assertion. The incident was credited with breaking the taboo against female cigarette smoking in public, and the practice was both normalized and valorized. It was normalized because women of high social standing were seen to do it without shame, and it was valorized through the association with feminine freedom and the values of America.

Bernays enjoyed similar success with many other corporate clients. His ideas on crowd psychology and the manipulation of public opinion through the news, rather than through advertising, were compelling. Marketing has slowly caught up with Bernays, as the persuasive force of publicity techniques such as sponsorship and product placement have gradually been realized and absorbed into mainstream marketing practice. The merging of PR and marketing techniques has been accelerated and assisted by the convergence of media platforms and the wide availability of movies, news media, and TV shows, which can be viewed on the same device. Bernays was acutely conscious of the value of audience activation, and he understood well that leveraging an idea through more than one communication channel (sometimes known as Integrated Marketing Communications today) had a particular value. Bernays also understood that audiences need not be bashed over the head with hegemonic, loud-hailer messages. At that New York Easter Parade he orchestrated a mise-en-scéne effect that was both brazen, and cunning. The success of this gambit depended on Bernays's deep understanding of the cultural context. He understood how the press worked, he understood the authority and reach of TV and cinema newsreels, and he appreciated the symbolic force of the debutante's cigarette smoking statement in the context of US social class. The debutantes were young, expensively educated women from wealthy families, and they had a quasi-celebrity status as leaders of feminine style and manners.

Bernays would not have categorized his approach as marketing or advertising. He was, according to accounts, focused on promoting the distinct discipline of public relations as a social science of mass influence, with himself at the head of it. My aim in relating his story is not to conflate different communication disciplines but to illustrate the need for a fully contextual understanding in order to appreciate the mise-en-scéne character of marketing dynamics in a convergent media environment. Today, product and service brands are consistently cross-referenced, implicitly and explicitly, in news and entertainment media brands. Marketing, which I see as a catch-all term embracing all the promotional disciplines, operates at an ideological level, normalizing and valorizing brands as taken-for-granted accessories to everyday life, and as symbols of identity. Bernays understood the particular social influence of news media and authority figures, but he could hardly have anticipated the extent to which, some 70 years later, commercial interests, invariably branded for recognition, would seep into a thoroughly integrated media environment. Marketing and entertainment have become news, while news is sold as entertainment. The Dr Dre, *Oreos* and *Bodyform* examples were ineluctably marketing initiatives, but they eschewed conventional marketing and mainlined straight into new media. The *Labour isn't Working* example, in contrast, had to become talked about the old fashioned way, through luck.

## MARKETING AND PR IN A CONVERGENT MEDIA ENVIRONMENT

Some people might feel that there is something sinister and insidious about Bernays's approach to brand marketing. My feeling is that it is important for citizens, students and practitioners to recognize how marketing really works, whether or not one feels it is right. The integrated and interlocking marketing-media-entertainment-news industry, a postmodern culture industry[22] if you will, has been realized through the liberalization of media controls, horizontal and vertical mergers in the media industry and advances in digital media. It is, simply, a fact of contemporary life. The more we understand of its operation the better we can negotiate our lives through the self-referential morass of commercially infused media communication. Informed consumers make more efficient markets, and stronger democracies.

Marketing, as any introductory text book will aver, entails more than communication. It may be closely identified with advertising and promotion by the general public, and with public relations by me, but matters such as distribution, pricing, manufacture and product development, design and service are hardly insignificant. I do feel, though, that a focus on communication issues can be highly instructive, partly because of the way the entire marketing effort is distilled in communication. A typical consumer will encounter only the communication tip of the marketing iceberg. All the values and ideas of the marketing effort are condensed into that momentary consumer experience. All too often, communication is dismissed in marketing as a frivolous accessory to the real grunt of supply chain and product management, production, sales and merchandising, and the rest. I concede that advertising is my own main point of reference in marketing, and like most marketing academics I have a bias toward FMCG[23] marketing because of its scale, resources and visibility. I would argue, though, that a tendency to treat communication as a flighty and enigmatic afterthought in the marketing process has inflected a great deal of theorizing on all areas of marketing, to their detriment. The market metaphor is primarily a medium of communication, and the processes of stocking, price negotiation and display are secondary.

If Bernays's approach to promotion based on ideology (or, if you prefer, propaganda) is deemed beyond the scope of marketing, then what of the ideological enterprise that is marketing itself, as conceived in countless elementary text books and courses?[24] Conventional books and courses about marketing can be seen as part of an ideological enterprise focused around Harvard University and Boston-based consulting companies, promoting the idea that organizations operate as the servants of a commercial democracy in which the consumer is sovereign and marketing is open, rational and transparent. Bernays would not have had to flip through very many pages of a typical marketing text book to recognize that these mass-selling tomes are pure PR. Arguing in favour of a more inclusive scope for marketing may risk conflating or minimizing the distinctions between different marketing techniques, but I'd argue that this is a risk worth taking if it can achieve a more fruitful and insightful engagement with the subject.

The examples above illustrate not only the connectedness, through social media, that runs through contemporary marketing business models, but also the force with which communication is able to symbolize the marketing thinking as a microcosm of the all the ideas and actions that have gone into the brand. This is not to suggest that consumers form a complete and final view of a brand from in a single ad exposure – clearly this is seldom so. Nonetheless, I think communication strategy can be a bellweather for the coherence and cogency of the entire marketing effort, or for the lack of it. Communications can express strategic thinking with an economy and import that no other element of marketing can match, so it can be particularly instructive to try to unravel the dynamics at play when consumers and communications engage.

## THE LANGUAGE OF MARKETING IN ORGANIZATIONS

So much of the art of marketing entails the carefully crafted use of words, one can forget that marketing work itself is also about language. I've already touched on the artfully constructed, yet often taken-for-granted, tropes of the managerial marketing textbook genre. As I've asserted in the previous chapter, expert professionals' experiences of marketing work tend to be articulated in a very different style, and with a rather different vocabulary. I've spoken to many experienced marketing practitioners in the course of my research. They seem to me to have two things in common. One is their passion for the work, conveyed with an earnestness that belies the cynical public perception of marketing folk. They are, no doubt, ambitious and driven, but many have an impressive commitment to the quality of work. They are excited by their place in the engine room of popular consumer culture, and they want to leave their creative stamp on the field. The other thing they have in common is the lack of jargon invoked when they talk about their daily workplace activities. Most speak articulately and insightfully but they seldom express themselves in marketing text book verities. They've gone a long way past the very basic vocabulary provided by the books. Their talk about their experience is nuanced, contingent and contextual. They know that in marketing management there are no magic bullets, and the text book theories don't work. I'm impressed by the fluid, connected and non-technical yet compelling way in which many experts talk about their professional practice in marketing because of the way it articulates a pragmatic and contingent world-view. They seem to express what in academic jargon might be called a socially constructed ontology of practice. There are no algorithms and no fixed points in their experiential world of work. In a perpetually shifting marketing environment, practitioners operate in a world of Einsteinian relativity, not Newtonian mechanics.

This lack of jargon tends to carry through from talk *about* marketing work to the talk involved *in* marketing work.[25] For example, in advertising, the account planner will distil the communication strategy into an advertising strategy expressed in a way "your Mum could understand." This will then be used in a creative brief that encapsulates the consumer and market insight and dovetails with the client's marketing strategy.[26] I admit that my own use of language might sometimes be a little exotic for non-academic readers, but I am very taken with the idea that marketing does not need to rely on its abstract technical concepts but can be conveyed in educated but ordinary language. Experienced practitioners I have encountered graduate from the broad and static terms of elementary marketing textbooks to a highly personalized expression that often makes use of vivid metaphors and novel turns of phrase. Marketing professionals need to demonstrate expert communication skills in order to fulfill their internal organizational tasks of advocacy and education, and many are able to do this across disciplinary boundaries because of their linguistic fluency.

I'm not ignoring those hoards of marketers involved in more technical activities involving databases, algorithms and ROI (return on interest) calculations, all of which form essential components to marketing's sweeping scope as an organizational function. Technical jargon serves a purpose as convenient shorthand for people who operate in the same milieu, but many more marketing folk face a task of articulating marketing within and across the organization to connect with people with very different disciplinary backgrounds, educations and work roles. What is more, they have the task of articulating marketing priorities to customers and other stakeholders. In my admittedly small sample of experience, they tend to do it very well as advocates.

In this sense, marketing professions, like most other professions that involve speaking and advocacy, benefit from an understanding of the rhetoric of persuasion. Other marketing writers[27] have drawn attention to the point that marketing work may often be represented as a technical discipline of behavioral science, but the daily tasks of a marketing professional typically revolve around the use of language. Marketing professionals compose and write market research reports, advertising copy and business analysis reports, they debate and argue for different courses of action at meetings, they write strategy documents, brochure copy and reports, they make pitch presentations, conduct sales presentations – the list could go on. Within organizations, as well as in customer interactions, the day-to-day work of marketing is very substantially focused around the deployment of language and communication.

Clarity is a virtue but obfuscation can also serve a purpose, since obtuse language is a potent rhetoric of persuasion in itself. The language of marketing has become a symbol of organizational power and authority. Calls for better customer service, for example, have become a motif for the control of call centre and other service staff, while strategy documents and mission statements are often used as benchmarks against which to measure the behavior of employees. Indeed, marketing has become identified with the language of bluster, bombast and many other grades of BS precisely because of its role as a distinctively *political* activity in negotiating power battles within the organization and persuading, mollifying or counseling consumers and stakeholders beyond it. I would argue, though, that marketing strategy development is best served through a nuanced use of language that prises open the closed categories of marketing concepts to engage with the particular contextual detail of marketing situations. There is nothing wrong with better customer service, but achieving it is rarely helped by closing down input over exactly how it can be achieved.

## DIGITAL COMMUNICATION AND THE MARKETING CONCEPT

As some of this chapter's examples have shown, the internet has opened up the plausible tautology of the marketing concept and given consumers a voice, when formerly they were mere segments in a board room pie chart. The ideology that marketing serves society and organizations alike by aligning consumer needs and wants with organizational resources, has been enduring, but it is no less hypothetical than the economists' notion of perfect competition. There are countless examples of marketing flair that seem to run counter to marketing principles about researching, and then serving, latent needs and wants, despite the valiant attempts of case writing houses to suggest otherwise.[28] Internet-based business models, in particular, tend to be ineluctably Fordist in the sense that the idea comes first, and the consumers follow. In a most un-Fordist way, the business case tends to be made for internet brands after everything else has been set up. Internet brands have up-ended orthodox marketing principles by giving their service away free of charge, then devising novel ways of generating revenue streams. In the success of Amazon, YouTube, Facebook, Twitter and many more, consumers were not consulted on their needs and wants before marketing strategists devised ways to serve those needs. The great idea was originated without any assistance from consumers or marketing principles, then the word spread and the internet traffic grew. Facebook and YouTube, for example, began as the brainchildren of nerdy kids who wanted to make their own social lives more fun. They discovered that a lot of other people wanted to join in, and the sites grew. After years of development, they started to think about making money. The logic of the internet is "build traffic, and worry about revenue later."

But there is a twist to the way the internet has inverted the traditional text-book marketing concept of seeking out consumer needs, then satisfying them profitably. Production can be outsourced to the consumer, and marketing has seamlessly merged with applied communication. These internet brands exemplify the interactivity of new business models – the public *makes* the brand in a far reaching sense through their daily interactions with it. This immaterial labor is supplied free of charge, in exchange for a consideration – the free use of the service. These brands did not serve pre-existing customer needs, any more than the Sony Walkman did in the 1980s when, against the advice of his market researchers, Sony CEO Akio Morita insisted on putting Walkmans on the shelves of Sony stores. They re-configured those needs entirely with a new offer that was beyond the imagination of consumers. Today's digital Fordism has consumers virtually walking around the factory and contributing to the production process.

Most marketing offers today have some interface with electronic communications, in the form of an internet presence. Consequently they have to take account of the cultural contexts in which these communications will be received. For marketing organizations, the internal logic that drives ideas can seem compelling, but the internet means they are opened up to scrutiny at every stage by a relentlessly probing public and media. This presents acute difficulties of representation and interpretation. There may be an internal sense of what constitutes the key components of the marketing offer, but conveying this externally through a website or any other medium demands a strong sense of how the offer might be interpreted and understood by external audiences, as the examples in this chapter demonstrate. The internet and social media have created fields of engagement in which organizational activities, offers and values are instantly judged. A sharp understanding of the entire context of the market and the consumer, and especially of the communication aspects, is more indispensible to marketing organizations than ever.

## THE CONSUMER "DECISION"

Marketing effects on consumers are often assumed to result from single elements in the consumer environment, such as an exposure to an advertisement, a price reduction, an appealing logo, attractive packaging or an appealing feature of the product. The examples above show that, in order to understanding marketing fully, the different levels of operation must be considered. What I call the cognitive paradigm in marketing management is broadly the assumption that buying decisions rest on an individual, rational response to a decisive stimulus. This focuses on one level of consumer consciousness, the cognitive, but it ignores the wider cultural context. Large-scale consumer brand marketing is only partly about persuading people consciously and rationally to change their individual buying decisions – it's far more powerful and significant purpose is to frame consumer choices to make buying decisions redundant. In other words, it is about setting the consumption scene so that what takes place seems to do so with self-evident rationality. Bernays's vision of social control through public relations was not so far from advertising and marketing as he claimed. After all, big business was once considered anti-American because it destroyed the little main street trader, until the ad agencies stepped in to anthropomorphize the corporations[29] and, in so doing, legitimized big business. Now, they stand as symbols of the American Way, when once they were its antithesis. Our cultural predispositions lie deeper than our cognitive mechanisms. The latter, indeed, are often predetermined by the former. Emotion is socially constructed, and marketing is the discipline that taps into these cultural strains of behavior.

In this chapter I've tried to point to some of the ways in which marketing communication can be conceived as something that is far wider in scope and more complex in its effects that traditional marketing communication models, like AIDA, allow. In particular, I've tried to link the macro level of marketing communication, where Bernays's PR operated, and the micro level, where you or I feel that we've made a decision about a purchase. The two levels, I think, operate inter-dependently to constitute the consumer cultural mise-en-scéne.

# CHAPTER 3

# Marketing Ideology and Mass Media

## PR AND THE CULTURAL MISE-EN-SCÉNE

From a consumer perspective, marketing stands for color, creativity, and cunning; it is glitzy, ritzy, dirty, flirty, and fun. But, it is also an important subject of study in view of its economic impact and pervasive social influence. Popular understanding of marketing's ideas has permeated through to political, public sector and policy bodies, and in this role marketing's assumed value often seems unquestioned and beyond critique. I want to make a case here for a contextual approach to understanding marketing techniques and effects, on managerial, policy, and also educational grounds. As part of this effort, I also want to promote a critical and demystified understanding of this enigmatic topic. To try to do this I will touch on a selection of ideas from literary theory and cultural studies that are not typically invoked in how-to marketing books.

As I noted in Chapter 2, Edward Bernays felt that public relations operated on a more sophisticated, ideological level, compared to marketing and advertising. For Bernays, PR set the consumer cultural scene. Marketing and advertising sold the seats. I refer to ideology here not in a party political sense, but to mean, broadly, the communication of values and ways of understanding the world that are represented as being self-evident and neutral, but which, in fact, support particular interests. Mass media operate as particularly powerful vehicles for ideology because they occupy intimate roles in the lives of consumers, presenting brands and consumption in everyday settings. Through its role in promotional culture,[1] marketing normalizes consumption as a taken-for-granted part of life. At the same time as they normalize consumption, though, mass media invest in it a frisson of glamour. In other words, consumption becomes valorized as a signifier of status, success, and happiness. News, documentary, education, and information are presented on the same media platforms as entertainment. Techniques of presentation leak across genres, and the context frames the interpretation. Bernays's PR stunt had an ideological character in the sense that it resulted in women smoking cigarettes being reported as "news," when in fact the incident was a carefully designed promotional stunt. At the time, cigarette smoking by men was common in Hollywood movies and advertising, and it had, hence, already been invested with symbolic meaning. Cigarette smoking was a sign of a person who was a socially assured individualist who went against the grain of convention. A slight adjustment of the mise-en-scéne was needed to legitimize the habit for women.

Bernays's view seemed to be that marketing operates at ground level, inducing consumers to swap brands or to spend a little more on self-indulgence with utility-based appeals to consumer rationality. He felt that PR, in contrast, operates on a loftier plane, framing the entire world-view of the population through the influence of news media. Macro and micro influence, if you will. In the 1940s, some other cultural currents were already shifting slowly toward greater independence for women, since the war had broken down many gender barriers in workplaces. This social shift, though, created cultural tension with traditional patriarchal values, and cigarette smoking was a way of resolving this symbolically, giving women the symbol of independence when, in fact, their lives were in many respects still as oppressed as before. Bernays understood that consumption is an emotional and symbolic experience. He exploited the authority of influential opinion-formers[2] in his PR strategies with the aim of getting people to internalize the role of marketing and consumption as a taken-for-granted reference point in their lives, and as an intimate part of one's identity. Whether a woman chose to smoke *Lucky Strike* cigarettes or *Camel* was relatively trivial, and could be left to the marketers to fight over. Bernays was working for the makers of *Lucky Strike*, but he understood the problem on an ideological level as an issue of the cultural meaning of smoking. The important decision, to smoke cigarettes, had already been made, thanks to Bernays's astute understanding, and manipulation, of the cultural mise-en-scéne.

There is a nice speech in the movie *The Devil Wears Prada* on the topic of consumer choices being pre-determined. The Miranda Priestly character, played by Meryl Streep, mocks her assistant Andy Sachs's view that her "choice" of an unfashionable sweater set her beyond the dictats of the fashion industry. Priestly, assumed to be based on *Vogue* editor Anna Wintour, explains that Sachs's "lumpy" sweater is not blue, but "cerulean," and Sachs would not have had the opportunity to buy it from some marked-down clearance shelf in a provincial store if it had not been for the cerulean ranges major designers like *Yves Saint Laurent* and Oscar de la Renta displayed at major fashion shows years before. Priestly/Streep asserts that what Sachs thinks is her anti-high fashion "choice" is in fact the result of the investment and talent of the very industry she disdains.[3]

The fashion business, of course, relies heavily on PR to frame the choices that high street fashion consumers think they're making. Links with fashion journalists and celebrity agents are central to the development of fashion brands.[4] The PR element of this could be described as ideological in the sense that world views, in this case, aesthetic judgments about particular fashion collections, are presented as if they are neutral and independent, but in fact they support the interests of a particular group.[5] The fashion journalists who make or break labels through their reviews see themselves as independent opinion formers. The suggestion that PR has ideological effects does not necessarily imply that there is overt corruption or self-conscious manipulation. Media professionals are susceptible to marketing influence in ways which may well be unwitting, as we can see from Bernays's example. What is more, values and opinions are often internalized unreflexively in group settings. The judgments we voice have a social character. The journalists and newsreel makers who covered the New York Easter Parade of 1939 were, presumably, reporting events in good faith, unaware that the cigarette protest was not a genuine political statement but a publicity stunt paid for by big tobacco. Perhaps these were more innocent times – or perhaps some press men were in on Bernays's scheme too. Fashion journalists, film critics, and other arbiters of public taste may work independently but they operate within a milieu. They also have editorial masters – fashion labels that advertise heavily in style magazines tend to enjoy favorable editorial. It's just the way the world works.

Bernays's brand of PR was more subtle than, say, the kind where celebrity stories are traded to publications that publish them even though are likely to be false. This is perhaps where there is a line between PR and propaganda. Propagandists have a political purpose to their lies. Publishers of false celebrity stories have a more pragmatic aim, to sell a magazine. PR is a communication profession that is undertaken in good faith, but sometimes untrue stories are created to meet the public demand for celebrity sensation. The funneling of false consumer choices through selective media representations might be thought benign – what does it matter if a few consumers buy a magazine because they believe an untrue celebrity story? A magazine has been sold, and some readers have enjoyed a few minutes distraction for a small cost. The celebrity might well have even earned a fee for the story, as well as benefiting from the exposure. Being a media celebrity today has become a profession in itself, and staying in the public eye is the key. In the UK, an out-of-work soap actress can eat like a horse for a few months, have an unflattering bikini photograph taken, then hire a personal trainer, lose the weight, and sell the story as an advertisement for the exercise DVDs and the angsty biography. It's absurd, and it's as much marketing as it is PR. Celebrities can be commoditized as brands, and the brand can be extended through DVDs, books, and celebrity media stories, as well as through the celebrity's core business (if they have one) of performing.

As for Bernays, he may have had an ethical blind spot, but he probably didn't know cigarette smoking would have catastrophic public health implications. It was just a job for a client. On a wider scale one could argue, though, that this kind of shady PR undermines the public faith in media integrity in general, and contributes to a cycle of cynicism in which media vehicles produce stories that are untrue for people who don't believe them but read them anyway for sensational or prurient entertainment. The numbers of citizens who engage regularly with the less sensational news media have been falling drastically for decades. A majority of citizens in Western democracies seem not to engage regularly with news media at all. As sales fall, the sensationalism and entertainment-orientation of the media increases in an effort to keep a market share of a dwindling audience. In the UK, for example, with a population of just over 60 million, the biggest circulation daily newspaper is the overtly populist and entertainment-oriented *The Sun*, with daily sales of just 2.5 million or so. The second biggest seller is the *Daily Mail*, which also enjoys the most popular newspaper website in the world, with more than 100 million unique users a day visiting for a diet of florid human interest stories and strident political comment.[6] The old "broadsheets" with their wordy geo-political analyses and drab visual layout, seem to be going the way of the dinosaurs.

## BLURRING LINES BETWEEN MARKETING AND PR

What interests me here is not simply the dynamic of media in influencing and reflecting public opinion, but the ways in which marketing, consumption, and brands are increasingly inter-twined into this process. For example, the biggest show on UK commercial TV in recent years has been *X Factor*.[7] The old TV talent show format was revived and refreshed by Simon Cowell, who turned it into an entertainment Leviathan that has become a global franchise. As I write, the show in the UK seems to have passed its peak and real-time audiences for the 2012 series fell below 11 million, a couple of million down from its heyday. The public has grown weary of the formula and the show is looking tired. Nonetheless, it was credited with reviving the UK's commercial broadcaster ITV by ramping up advertising revenue when it had been falling through the floor just a few years before. The show sits at the centre of a marketing enterprise that includes multiple revenue streams through costly phone-in audience voting, a free website that also retails paid-for downloads of perform-ances and the contestants' latest song releases, while the site also acts as an advertisement for the spin-off live shows, and for the show itself. There was also an *X Factor* magazine for a while, there is paid-for product placement within the TV show, repeated on clips on the website and on YouTube, and the show as a whole is a placement vehicle for new and old songs and artists, often run by the same management companies. This concoction is heated up by a stream of PR stories fed to an eager celebrity news media. UK newspapers friendly to the show feature *X Factor* stories day-after-day during the show's run. *X Factor* is ineluctably a marketing enterprise that succeeds in activating engagement with the brand and monetizing social media traffic.[8] Make no mistake, *X Factor* may be a media brand but this is the quintessence of contemporary marketing – it isn't so much an entertainment show as a piece of expensively crafted branded content,[9] and the audience engagement is, to a considerable extent, driven by PR.

The *X Factor* spin machine rolls into action during the early televised auditions, when some wannabee stars' lamen-table singing skills are mercilessly, and publicly, trashed by the judges. The contestants who fly off the handle and hurl abuse at the judges often make the national press in the UK, with stories lambasting the cruelty of the show, and/or the emotional instability of some contestants. The PR for the live shows featuring the finalists usually revolves around alleged squabbles between the celebrity judges or the carefully crafted rags-to-possible-riches stories of the contestants. In fact, the format bears more than a passing resemblance to a ritual rite of passage, a similarity me and my colleagues pointed out in a research paper that itself attracted a fair bit of media coverage.[10] We argued that the way the quintessential media marketing brand of the age, *X Factor*, exploits the collective need for rite-of-passage rituals can be seen in many other brands too. Marketing often sells a sense of the possibility of personal transformation that may be vicarious, and illusory, but has a powerful appeal, nonetheless.[11]

Bernays's view that PR is the superordinate discipline of public influence was based on the assumption that news media had a unique authority. No doubt, this remains the case despite the relatively small audience figures for news, but the media environment today has changed much since the black and white cinema newsreel coverage of the 1930s. Digital communications technology, changing media consumption patterns, and horizontal mergers have blurred the lines between different media outlets to create a seamless complex of news, marketing, and entertainment. As we can see from news audience and circulation figures, many people access little or no dedicated "news" media, and many others access news coverage only through entertainment vehicles like MSN, or hybrid news-entertainment vehicles like the *MailOnline*. News media vehicles themselves are packaged and sold (to advertisers and subscribers) as marketed media brands. That doesn't imply that they are, necessarily, inherently, or system-atically propaganda outlets, by any means. The selection and presentation of news is filtered through the news vehicle's own brand positioning, the agenda of its journalists and editorial team, and the political and class prejudice of its readers, listeners, or viewers. In other words, newspapers and TV news shows are marketed brands, located within contextualized consumer markets and framed by interlocking global media interests. Other issues influencing editorial decisions in media include the corporate cross-promotion required by the news brand's ownership structure, and the power of advertisers to tacitly influence editorial agenda. This influence does not necessarily impugn journalistic integrity, but it acts behind the scenes to give order to the selection and composition of news stories.

Added to this, many cash-strapped press vehicles have imposed economic savings by reducing the number of journalists and downplaying the role of investigative journalism in favour of publishing pieces fed to them by news and PR agencies. This latter element has assumed increased importance since readership, listener, and viewer figures for many media vehicles shrank and fragmented, so that celebrity gossip and sensationalized news coverage became a key marketing tool for media brands. There is still courageous independent journalism, but the huge and growing influence of PR and lobbying from celebrity agents, industry, and political lobbyists is also apparent in the shaping of the contemporary media infrastructure. All this means that news media and editorial are more susceptible than ever to commercial influence through lobbying and PR, or, as I'd call it, marketing.

## CONTEXT AND "CONTENT" MARKETING

My point, with this digression into media studies, is that the consumer cultural context in which marketing operates has changed in the past 50 years. Bernays saw that news media wield a powerful mise-en-scéne effect that is vulnerable to commercial influence, but, today, media editorial, including news, is more intimately connected than ever before to entertainment, marketing, and commercial interests in general. News coverage has become sucked into a wider ideological complex, a marketing-media-news-entertainment culture industry,[12] perhaps. The linkages between marketing and media might be obvious to most (whether or not this constitutes a "culture industry") but they are barely acknowledged in managerial marketing or advertising studies. PR techniques such as placing branded products into entertainment and news media, or others such as "sponsorship," celebrity endorsement, and "plugging" of brands on mass and social media, have become absorbed into the accepted scope of marketing as elements of the promotional mix. As the lines between promotion and editorial become harder to see, mediated news and entertainment become potential content for marketing. Marketing orthodoxy holds that elements of the promotional mix have quite different characteristics. Advertising, for example, carries offers that consumers are free to evaluate and reject, and this is alleged to be quite distinct from media editorial. The orthodox view on new media is that they exert a powerful democratizing effect on marketing by giving consumers a voice. The truth, in both cases, is more nuanced, and the already hackneyed term of "content" may be useful for bridging the different categories of promotion.

"Content marketing" is touched upon in the more avant garde marketing text books but the treatment of it often focuses narrowly on social, rather than mass, media. Content marketing stands apart from advertising and, instead, develops brand stories, primarily for exposure in social media, by engaging with consumers through entertainment. *Coca Cola*, for example, succeeded in turning their content marketing strategy into a piece of content marketing, by putting engaging videos of their strategy on YouTube.[13] Other brands have created mini movies, one of the most notable examples being *BMW*'s famous series of car-chase capers called *The Hire* and starring actor Clive Owen. These movies have been viewed over 100 million times and are credited with tangible sales increases for the cars,[14] not to mention the boost they allegedly gave to Owen's own career. More recently, *Jaguar* got into the act with their 2013 movie *Desire*, made to launch their first new sports car in 50 years, the F Type.[15] Branded content on mass media is nothing new – the first "soap operas" on American TV in the 1950s were general entertainment shows made entirely to showcase the sponsor's products, and this style of sponsored TV programming is beginning to make a comeback today. What is new is that growth in social media and mobile technology, and those changing media consumption patterns, have increased the opportunities for branded content that is produced as entertainment. In the *BMW and Jaguar* movies, the car is the real star, but the movies contain no overt promotion at all. They don't need to. The movies are exciting extended car chases. Nothing else needs to be said. These promotional vehicles seem like nothing so much as free entertainment, since consumers have become so used to actual movies prominently featuring branded props. Many consumers, and the majority of younger ones, have no problem at all with the presence of brands in entertainment and, in fact, expect it.[16] For brands, a specially made movie is not much more costly than a prominent placement in a major movie, with the added benefits of full creative control and ownership of the intellectual property in the movie. While media regulators and some advocates of public service broadcasting might agonise over the separation of editorial and advertising, most viewers are less concerned as long as their entertainment looks right. Dramatic realism has become the accepted norm in TV entertainment. Scenes bereft of branded content seem artificial and lacking in the verisimilitude that audiences demand. In turn, many TV advertisements are now produced as mini-movies, with the brand featuring in a major, but implicit role. What all this means is that media genres seem to be collapsing into each other, as more advertising looks like entertainment, and more entertainment looks like advertising.

The concept of content marketing is ineluctably an ideological strategy, since it seeks to valorize and normalize the brand as an intimate part of consumers' lives in a way that is constituted as entertainment, rather than as overt promotion. Car producers' primary purpose and duty is to sell cars, not to provide expensive entertainment that is free for drivers and non-drivers alike to enjoy. Content marketing strategies are not confined to movie making but also include paid journalists writing for brand blogs and the creation of games around brands (called game-ification, or advergaming). "Content" marketing has many advantages over conventional mass media promotion. For example, content is available 24/7 on the internet, so there is no need for conventional media planning as with "bought" media space. Content also suits the convergent media environment. Media engagement, especially through mobile devices, has become a feature of everyday life in affluent and also not-so-affluent countries. Using a mobile phone is an intimate part of millions of lives, and for many their phone is never more than an arm's length away. The mobile phone is the most potent promotional device yet known, and it is a medium that suits content more than it suits advertising. The provision of branded content than can be accessed on mobile devices opens up potential audiences of hundreds of millions.

## SALES EFFECTS OF CONTENT MARKETING

The marketing logic of branded content is that mediated entertainment showcases brands in everyday settings while also enhancing their prestige. Through this kind of presence brands can become part of the cultural vocabulary, which makes it easier for them to enter the consumers' "evoked set." The evoked set represents the six or seven alternatives from which we typically make purchase decisions, since working memory only holds about this number of items. Miller's "magic number 7" is well known in psychological studies of memory, after psychologist George A. Miller, but rarely earns a mention in marketing theory. Nonetheless, it is a feature of consumer behavior since most purchases are made against the range of alternatives we can easily recall. Translate that into audiences of many millions, and it is clear that a brand that makes it into the working memory of consumers, and into the evoked set of potential purchases, is likely to sell in large numbers, provided the ease of recall is matched by the ease of purchase. There is no need for persuasion, or for a sales pitch, as such. If you're a little hungry, you like chocolate, and you're near a confectionary sales outlet in the UK, it's either a *Mars*, *Twix*, *Snickers*, *Kit Kat*, *Bounty*, erm, *Cadbury's Dairy Milk*, and that's all I've got. Do they still sell *Milky Way*? *Crunchy*? It's been a while since I ventured into a candy shop. For regular purchasers, the choice has already been framed through large scale marketing budgets, and the brands occupy a familiar place in our everyday, habitual worlds.

Cultural presence is by no means the only component of marketing success, but it seems to be a precondition for "iconic" brands.[17] According to Douglas Holt, iconic brands tap into cultural myths, so *Coca Cola* became the taste of America, *Harley Davidson* a symbol of American freedom and *Budweiser* beer the drink of the honest American blue collar worker. For Holt, the stories these brands tell resolve dilemmas of American identity. American provenance does not confer the prestige on brands that it once did, and global brands have to negotiate a different kind of consciousness that extends beyond national borders. Brands constitute a shared symbolic vocabulary, a public language, and content marketing facilitates brand stories. The origin of the story, and its ulterior motive, may be understood, but it is left implicit, and that adds to the story's rhetorical force. We, the consumers, complete the narrative.

For marketers, maintaining market share by keeping the brand fresh, current, and present is a challenge. Getting consumers to change buying behavior is a much bigger one. For a new brand to enter an established market and squeeze into that evoked set takes more than novel advertising and massive marketing resources. It requires a change in the consumers' frame of reference, brought about by a change in the composition of the mise-en-scéne. The brand has to engage, to become part of the consumer cultural vocabulary. This demands creativity and craft, grounded in an acute sensitivity to the consumer cultural context. The sales effect is indirect, but potentially all the more powerful for that. As consumers, we're looking for distractions from the dilemmas of our human condition. Entertainment and marketing are perfect partners for providing these.

## CONTENT AND EPISODIC MEMORY

Another psychological factor in the marketing value of branded content is episodic memory. Humans aren't very good at recalling facts, which is why, if we are asked in a survey which brands of crisps we ate last month, or how many alcoholic drinks we drank last night, we seldom really know, so we take a rough guess. Our memories are far more effective at recalling experiences of lived episodes in our lives than facts. We might not be able to remember the name of a movie even though we remember scenes from it, and we might not remember which year it was when we had that wonderful holiday with the kids, but we might have vivid recollection of days on the beach. The force of episodic memory might explain some of the efficacy of content marketing. The brand is not necessarily recalled immediately after an encounter with branded content. Many consumer research tests used in the advertising business focus on semantic memory, which refers to those things we can explicitly recall on demand. The consumer is asked which brands he or she can remember after seeing the ad (or the content). Brand clients like semantic recall, because it's something that can be measured and put into bar graphs. The assumption is that, if the brand is recalled, then it was noticed. If it was noticed, it might be bought. Of course, it might not be bought at all, but at least the client has what they presume to be an intermediate measure of the effectiveness of their promotion. This reasoning also applies to the logic of AIDA – if the consumer pays enough attention to get interested, then perhaps they'll buy.

Semantic recall of a brand, though, doesn't tell the client anything about the context of recall. The consumer might recall it because they hated the way it was portrayed. For example, in product placement (where a brand is used in entertainment as a scene prop or script reference), recall scores tend to be higher where the placement is incongruous and doesn't fit with the plot or characterization. So, say, where Michael Douglas asked his co-star in *Wall Street 2010* whether he'd like a *Heineken* instead of just asking him whether he'd like a drink, movie-goers didn't like it. This kind of clunky placement annoys movie goers if it isn't done with humor and self-parody – they recall it because it clunked. So recall in itself can be a poor proxy for promotional effectiveness. Episodic memory is more difficult to conceptualize and measure than semantic memory, and consequently much less popular as a marketing ROI metric. But it potentially offers a more penetrating insight into the subtle ways branded content (including product placement) can integrate with the viewer's experience in a way that can be triggered at any time by that experience.

Experiences, including the experience of watching a video or TV show, can unconsciously be absorbed into episodic memory as narratives. They are only recalled when that story is triggered by another experience that maps on to the first, just as a smell of a birthday cake might make you think a day from your childhood. Police witness statements, for example, tend to rely on episodic memory, since a detective may ask a witness to recall everything that happened to them from the beginning of that day, hoping that recalling the context may trigger recall of specific details of an incident. Similarly, consumers interviewed about their experience of product placement in TV shows have told of events they later experienced that triggered the recall of the brand. In one case, walking into a *Dairy Queen* franchise triggered the memory of a soap opera character doing the same thing. The identification of life experiences with the heightened glamour of TV events, in association with actors or characters with whom viewers identify, adds to the salience.[18] Entertainment can be deeply relevant to peoples' lives. Episodic memories, and the limits of working memory, offer relatively simple psychological rationales for the way that content marketing, and the cultural presence it creates, might translate into purchases, assuming, of course, that the other elements of marketing are effectively in place and the brands are easily available to buy. Content marketing, then, like product placement or branded entertainment, can be seen as inherently ideological because its true purpose is masked. The fact that many or even most viewers may have enough commercial awareness to understand that purpose, does not render the communication non-ideological. The fact that the purpose is implicit, is enough.

Consumers do enjoy conventional mass media advertising when it's entertaining and relevant to them, but much advertising either annoys us because it isn't relevant to us, or it simply passes us by. There is a lot of it, and a great deal of it is not very interesting. "Content" consists in funny Facebook memes, stories in social media that are shared and elaborated, online videos such as the *Coca Cola* content strategy video or the *BMW* and *Jaguar* movies, online games built around brands, sponsored brand blogs, or other participatory media events in which the brand is present, in some way. Content marketing reflects the shift in media consumption patterns toward internet browsing for amusement. I think it also reflects a tacit and largely unarticulated acknowledgement in marketing practice that it's most powerful effect, is ideological. Designing an ideological marketing strategy requires a full understanding of the consumer cultural context, in order to develop content that is seen by the audience as compelling and relevant. In much the same way, a playwright, screenwriter, novelist or, indeed, an advertising copywriter, might need to have a finger on the cultural pulse in order to be able to express something that resonates with the collective consciousness. Through social media, content strategies evolve in interaction with consumers, as the content sparks a media conversation, which in turn suggests new content development ideas for the brand. This isn't a matter of crudely "crowd-sourcing" ideas, or even of community co-creation, because it involves a combination of iterative strategy, dialectical meaning-making, and creative cultural leadership. The consumers "read" the content and respond, as consumers. The marketers read the consumer responses, and feed that into strategy development. Only one of the two parties is operating as part of a conscious and well-resourced effort to promote the values of the brand.

## MARKETING AS PROPAGANDA?

It isn't the place here for a detailed interrogation of the putative distinctions between propaganda and Public Relations, but the topic is worth a brief note because of the ethical implications. If one accepts that the most powerful marketing effects are ideological, to what degree one ought to assume that the audience is sophisticated enough to bring a critical discernment to marketing's implicit persuasion? Should, or can, regulators protect the consumer from under-the-radar, ideological marketing?

Many consumers today are well-informed about the techniques of branded content, game-ification, adver-gaming, product placement, viral, advertorial, sponsorship, and celebrity endorsement, not to mention urban ideological strategies such as flash mobs, "pop-up" events, buzz and guerrilla marketing and the rest. These techniques have become widely accepted as relatively commonplace and, depending on the context, benign aspects of marketing and media, even though their commercial purpose is usually implicit rather than explicit. Ideological strategies have gone mainstream, not only in product branding but in service marketing, political marketing, social marketing, health, charities, and non-profit. Sometimes these strategies seem harmless, and even joyful – consider the *T-Mobile* flash mob at Liverpool Street Station in London, where scores of "commuters" suddenly began to dance in formation. This publicity stunt went viral (37 million YouTube views to date[19]) because it was such delightful fun.

Other examples of ideological marketing can be less joyful. While working for a major university some years ago (not my current employer), one of my students told me that he was a "brand ambassador" for a scotch whiskey manufacturer. This involved inviting friends around for free booze, provided by the company of course, and engaging his friends in discussion about it. All fairly straightforward for over-18s in the UK perhaps, until you find out that a company researcher is in attendance too. In this way the company was able to insinuate itself onto campus without the permission or knowledge of the university, to gather good quality consumer research data extremely cheaply, while also achieving its aim of broadening its consumer base to a younger group. My student was making some money and getting some valuable CV content to help his marketing career aspirations. Great for him, and relatively harmless for students who drink anyway, but ethical? Brand "ambassador" roles are common on campuses, and the ambassadors may not declare their interest when they are declaiming their passion for a particular brand, and encouraging their friends to use it. These brand propagandists are doing something that would be regarded as decidedly odd, if ideological marketing strategies had not become normalized as a benign game. My student's role as a double agent for a whiskey brand might be an exceptional example, although it is widely accepted that actors are sometimes hired to promote drinks brands in bars as if they are consumers, and it is also common knowledge that celebrities are sometimes paid to Tweet their praise of particular brands. The wide acceptance of marketing values has blunted social critique to such an extent that the distinction between propaganda and PR has been blurred. If the intent is commercial, then it is often regarded as benign by default.

Marketing cannot be properly understood without understanding the entire context of how consumer choices, predilections, fashions, and trends are framed at a macro as well as a micro level, with, it must be said, our willing complicity. But what are the deeper effects of this widespread ideological influence? Marketers are used to thinking of consumers as "savvy" and willingly engaged in the cat-and-mouse game of being persuaded. Marketers think like this because doing marketing well is very difficult. The best marketing is very clever indeed. Marketing jobs are usually demanding, insecure, and pressurised. Marketing professionals have to be astute and dedicated. Many consumers are sophisticated in the way they read marketing initiatives and marketers have to try to stay a step ahead.

But, there are also consumers who are less well-equipped to make critical judgments about the marketing to which they are subject. This includes not just vulnerable groups like children, the poor, the old, and the less well-educated, but otherwise highly capable people who have simply never thought of marketing in this way. A newspaper is a newspaper, right, a student party a student party, a funny video on YouTube just a funny video, and a movie a movie? Well, not any more buddy. If you haven't paid to watch, you're not an audience, you're a consumer.

## VANCE PACKARD AND MARKETING ETHICS

Some 50 years ago, Vance Packard's *The Hidden Persuaders*[20] alerted Americans to what Packard saw as the invidious use of "depth" psychology to reveal our hidden motivations, for exploitation by marketers. Much was made of "subliminal" advertising in broadcasting. This refers literally to messages of less than one sixteenth of a second inserted into movie reels so that they are only unconsciously seen. Subliminal advertising of this kind is not permitted by broadcasters, and in any case its effectiveness is an urban myth. But the term "subliminal" is now widely used as a general label for marketing that is implicit, rather than explicit, especially in ways people find sinister and manipulative. Packard tapped into a widespread suspicion of some techniques of marketing as forms of manipulation that are somehow wrong, underhand or unethical. Even though marketing techniques today are understood more widely than ever before, this unease, this sense that marketing is a dark and dishonest art, remains.

My observation that much of the most effective marketing practice utilizes techniques of propaganda and wields an ideological influence is not intended to condemn marketing and marketers. I am in favour of critical thinking and social critique, but not necessarily to promote a political ideology. As I see it, this is simply the truth about how marketing works. The ideological character of marketing seems to me to be deeply, and tacitly, understood in the contemporary advertising, branding, and marketing industries. It is part of pragmatic professional practice, yet it is unacknowledged in most managerial theory. It is not a veiled attack on capitalism to point out marketing's ideological character; it is just the way things are. It does, however, imply a social critique that places ethical responsibility on marketers. An understanding of context suggests that marketers cannot claim that they have no responsibility for the cultural implications of marketing practice – culture is their raw material. The priority on engagement that is implied in many ideological marketing strategies works both ways. It is designed to enhance the communication between brands and consumers, and implies that consumers must be listened to. I'm fascinated by how journalism, PR, and media influence work, and I've been addicted to news media all my life. I have even occasionally ventured into the murky realm of media exposure myself, with mixed results. I think it is a mistake to adopt a cynical view that, just because media are susceptible to commercial ideological influence, all media are tainted by hidden interests and therefore operate as a unified propaganda machine. Similarly, the view that all marketing (and marketers) are ethically bad is simplistic.

I feel there is a lot of integrity in news media but it seldom makes sense to rely on just one source, just as it make no sense to drink ten cans of cola per day. There is a continuum of cultural influence through media and individual action: structure and agency have a dialectical relation. Acknowledgement of the vested interests of media ownership networks, and the influence of PR lobbies and advertisers should, I think, form part of marketing education and training, since it certainly forms a big part of advanced marketing practice. This is the media infrastructure as it operates today, and it demands a well-informed engagement from consumers, as well as from practitioners. The ways that we engage with text, in its broadest sense as any form of representation, is central to our experience of contemporary consumer culture in a convergent media environment. We need to examine and critique not only the marketing texts we encounter, but also our responses to them. If we agree that marketing and entertainment are necessary to us, we need to cultivate more critically discerning forms of practice, and of consumer engagement.

Some years ago, when the university business school I was then working for decided it needed a stronger profile, I was introduced to a PR consultant hired by the university. I was organizing a seminar at the time, so the PR guy wrote up a piece about the seminar with quotes from me and a fun photo of me posing with a stack of branded packages. He put the piece on a press release database, and to my astonishment it was published verbatim, picture included, in the highly respected local newspaper, under a reporter's by-line. The piece was nice coverage for my department, and you could say it was a harmless short-cut for a hard-pressed reporter. It was news, of a kind, but it was hardly independent. It was, rather, a piece of branded content published under the guise of being editorial. Economic pressures on newsdesks must be causing even greater reliance on news agency and PR stories today. The article was a piece of marketing, but no one knew but the two of us, and the reporter. So, my PR guy and I were less than Bernaysian in our ambition. We didn't create a paradigm shift in the perception of our school, in fact I doubt anyone even read the piece, apart from the university PR office. But, I have been and continue to be a student of marketing, and if I was naive about this practice then, a lot of other people will be too. The assumption of consumer "savviness" cannot be assumed as a default position.

Media vehicles, then, are clearly powerful conduits for commercial influence. Marketing, broadly conceived as the promotion of consumption, is the unifying ideology. But it is mistaken, I believe, to identify the unquestionably totalizing effect of media influence with a unified or coherent system of media power. I think it is important to engage critically with media representations on a case-by-case basis and to try to pick apart the dynamics that led to particular representations emerging and becoming part of the discourse of a story, without succumbing to a general cynicism. Marketing isn't propaganda, but it does exert an influence on and through mass media that is largely ignored in marketing management theory. I don't feel that this implies a propaganda media model, or a liberal-pluralist one. As Herman and Chomksy[21] suggested, there is a dialectical process involved in the way media stories play out. There are internalized values that influence the media mise-en-scéne. There needs to be an ongoing conversation about, and awareness of, the dynamics of media in marketing, so that the wider public are kept up to speed with the media elites. My own instinct probably edges toward the liberal-pluralist end of the scale, where I'd favour a free speech assumption, with less regulation but more conversation, awareness, education, and critique. There clearly are, though, many exceptional cases that demand close attention, especially around the assumption of consumer "savviness" and vulnerable groups.

So, PR, as conceived by Bernays, has changed, and in some ways its influence is not only wider but more transparent. Many people read news and entertainment media with a baseline assumption that many stories connected with celebrities, entertainment, sport, and politics are spun by PR agencies and lobbyists. But the ways in which we engage with news media owes less to our presumptions about its independence, than to the mysteries of the text. Sometimes the most preposterous stories are able to generate tumultuous online comment simply because they are structured as "news." The discourse of news, the way it is presented rhetorically within a self-declared "news" medium, remains seductive for even the most cynical of readers. We read news as news, if it's framed as news, often without critically engaging with the content. The same applies for the textual arrangement of printed news. *The Sun* newspaper in Britain was a source of jokes about its comic book visual presentation (headlines in a font that took two-thirds of the page, vivid splashes of color, and playground word coinages) when it emerged in the 1970s. Back then, British TV comedian Ronnie Barker once remarked in a show that the main convenience of *The Sun* was that it read in the time it takes for a post-breakfast bathroom visit – "About two minutes." The line (in a show called *Porridge*) got a big canned laugh. No one in UK media laughs at *The Sun* any more. Its positioning to a market with a reading age of ten hasn't changed, but, as noted earlier, it is the biggest selling daily newspaper in the UK[22]). What is more, its proprietor Rupert Murdoch is credited with using it to make and break Prime Ministers, and it is treated as a "news" paper that has taken its place alongside organs of record like *The Times*, *The Telegraph*, and the rest.

As marketing becomes ever more closely entwined with media, I think it is sensible to acknowledge the role of marketing as an ideologically unified, but not conspiratorial, system of commercial promotion that inter-penetrates mass and social media. I think a critical engagement can serve a deeper and more contextually rounded understanding of the subject, and in turn that this should serve managers, students, citizens, and policymakers.

## ADVERTISING AS PR

Bernays, then, bracketed PR away from advertising and marketing, regarding them as weaker forms of persuasion. According to his argument, you thought you chose that sweater you're wearing because it appealed to your discerning aesthetic sense at the right price, but, like Andy Sachs, you were sadly mistaken. Your aesthetic sense is not yours at all, it was taught to you through fashion PR, and then the industry provided the products to serve the choice you'd been taught to make. Many American women were probably inspired by the news coverage of the 1939 Easter Parade to buy a pack of *Lucky Strike* and risk the disapproval of their menfolk by lighting up in a bar, or even at home. They perhaps felt that this was a deeply personal decision to do something, for once, for their own gratification, with which their men did not approve. But this personally liberating decision was not their own – their subjective and experiential worlds had been deeply penetrated by the much bigger world of news PR. For Bernays, PR set the scene for cultural norms. Marketing and advertising simply fed the illusion of choice. However, there is an argument that advertising operates in exactly the same way as PR.

The late Professor Andrew Ehrenberg, who spent most of his career debunking mistaken assumptions about statistical relationships in marketing and opinion research, argued that advertising seldom persuades us to buy a product or change our attitudes in the short term but, in fact, operates in the same way as publicity,[23] reminding us of the presence of a brand and reassuring us of its salience in our lives. Working from a very different intellectual tradition, critical media scholar Judith Williamson drew attention to the ideological character of advertising[24] as a semiotic system that frames and normalizes the way we understand brands in the world. For Ehrenberg, advertising is form of publicity, not of rational persuasion. Williamson also downplays the rational persuasion element, arguing that advertising has an ideological effect.

I'd argue that advertising's ideological effect, though, is not a form of one-way manipulation. Advertising is an essential element of the marketing system since it invests products and brands with cultural values and symbolic meanings, and it plays on its role not merely as a sales technique but as a form of social communication.[25] Advertising takes cultural values to reflect them back at us as the icing on a commercial offer, but it also invests culture with commercial values. Culture and economy are not separate entities: they make each other. This mutual constitution[26] means that advertising acts as a two-way mirror, reflecting between corporate commercial entities and the intimate psychological and physical spaces of everyday life. For example, *Coca Cola* advertising is sometimes thought to have influenced the visual representation of Santa Claus/Father Christmas through their adaptation of the image of a rotund man wearing a green outfit that was produced by another agency artist. *Coke*'s agency made St Nicholas into a fat man with a white beard who wore a red suit, and they gave it back to culture as the typical American representation of Santa Claus,[27] handily juxtaposed with a *Coke* logo. Similarly, the appellation "wassup" began life as an American English idiom, became the line in a *Budweiser* commercial, and then became an entry in Webster's dictionary. Advertising doesn't simply take its raw material from non-commercial culture like a cartoon vampire squid, sucking our autonomy and individuality to re-cast it all in terms of a sanitized and corporatized uniformity. It is part of the very same culture.

Williamson and Ehrenberg approached advertising using different methods and opposing intellectual traditions, but they reached some conclusions that shared a little common ground. For example, they might both have agreed that advertising doesn't "work" the way the marketing text books claim, like a mediated version of a salesperson persuading us to buy one brand instead of another. Rather, it sets the mise-en-scéne, cueing our very rationality, and making buying decisions trivial or irrelevant. Ehrenberg saw that "reminding" and "reassuring" are qualitatively different from persuading, and that the difference has far-reaching implications for management education and practice. If you will, it's a soft sell theory, which is still under-theorized in marketing curricula that are fixated on hard-sell, AIDA and hierarchy-of-sales effects. For her part, Williamson might have pointed out that "reminding" and "reassuring" are themselves cultural constructions that come about through the operation of capitalist ideology. So it may not be as easy as Bernays assumed, to bracket advertising away from PR as a brand-switching endeavour that is relatively trivial compared to PR's Big Picture influence. Advertisements, like branded content, draw on and reproduce ideologies, and hence they can be seen to operate in much the same way as PR.

## MARKETING SEMIOTICS

Williamson focused on the semiotics of advertising, the way that signs within advertisements produce meaning through representing something (icon), pointing to something (index), or symbolising something (symbol).[28] A smile, for example, might signify subservience, or shadenfraude, or acquiescence, flirtatiousness, affection, resignation, or any number of other things, depending on the confluence of other signs in a scene. Just as phonemes, the aural components of words, make no sense isolated from the surrounding context of a sentence, most signs have little meaning in the absence of other signs. The color red might signify different things in different contexts: stop, danger, good luck, embarrassment, pain. Advertisements can be seen as "strings of signs"[29] that are assembled to activate audiences. Semiotics, though, is far from being a unidirectional communication technique. Some versions of it do take a structural line, and assume that it operates according to fixed cultural codes, but others allow that the meaning of a sign is arbitrary, and culturally constructed. It is the audience who will deconstruct the meaning of the ad, so they must be regarded as complicit in meaning-making. The creator of the ad, therefore, must empathetically understand the audience's own cultural sign systems.

This need not mean that the ad must necessarily cohere with those systems. Sometimes, ads are contrived to be polysemic, in the sense that they leave open the possibility of multiple differing interpretations. To put this another way, you may not "get" the polysemic ad because it seems to make no sense. But there is nothing to get, other than that advertising is a semiotic game which, despite our occasional frustration or boredom with ads, we enjoy. For example, long-standing campaigns for *Diesel* clothing have used polysemy as a strategy to engage with their young, style-conscious target audiences,[30] and to confuse everyone else. The ads are constructed from bundles of images that almost mean something, but not quite. One I recall was set in a museum-like building with roped off exhibits and visitors, but it also had body builders wearing nappies or diapers, and a sort of space ship. The in-group know the joke – there is nothing to "get." The game is just to enjoy the fascination of watching the cogs turn in our own interpretive mechanisms. Polysemic ads engage us by drawing us into the game of inter-pretation. Advertisements operate as a unified mise-en-scéne in this sense, since they contain an artful array of signs that, together, work to engage consumers in the game of interpre-tation. According to linguist Guy Cook, advertising is a form of discourse that fulfils a need for textual play.[31]

Advertisements are by no means the only source of marketing signs. Marketing in general is the business of the management of meaning.[32] Marketing signs include the design and signage of a distribution outlet, the packaging, the visual design of the product, the physical setting for the service, the price, the location of the product within the supermarket, the juxtaposition with other products in the display, the livery of the corporate vehicles, the company letterheads, the look of the brochures, the look of the employees, the manner of the employees... you get the idea. And this is before we get into the interpretations consumers place on the brand through encounters with advertising, media coverage, merchandising, social media presence, and sales promotion. To the average consumer, the idea that marketing entails the interpretation of signs might seem more plausible when thinking of, say, rather abstract and arty fragrance, alcohol and fashion ads, than when thinking of more ostensibly prosaic ads for, say, financial services, toilet paper, detergent, car tyres, or breakfast cereals. However, the subtlety of ideological influence is that it plays on those very things that we do not notice, precisely because we take them for granted. Ideology is, also, the *process* by which we come to take certain things, values, ideas, visual representations, words, scenes, relations, for granted. Our particular semiotic deconstruction of the meaning of signs in juxtaposition has already been cued by our experience of the wider cultural mise-en-scéne.

Advertising, though, is not self contained. Julia Kristeva's concept of intertextuality has been used in advertising analysis[33] to articulate some of the ways in which advertising signs point to other signs outside the advertising text, linking advertising with wider culture. For example, a Frizzell insurance campaign I recall used news footage of iconic 1960s cultural events, against a '60s soundtrack, to signify its segmentation strategy to over '50s.[34] Common tropes in advertising refer to cultural discourses or ways of representing things, such as the grey-haired actor in the white coat drawing on the discourse of science to make claims about soap powder or medicines, the stereotypically happy family enjoying processed food, implying that the food brand is an integral component of a happy family life, or the animated salesman shouting directly into camera in a parody of a personal sales encounter. Ads often subvert cultural stereotypes, but this too has an inter-textual character, since the stereotype must be understood in order for the parody to hit home. For example, 2012 TV spots for *Heineken* beer parodied the James Bond action genre, with Daniel Craig himself appearing at the end in a knowing wink to the *Heineken* product placement in the Bond movie *Skyfall*. In short, advertising does not stand apart from other aspects of consumer culture, including, of course, mediated entertainment, and hence it is difficult to sustain an argument that advertising is fundamentally different in its mode of operation to PR or other forms of branded media content.

## MEDIA AND MARKETING IN CONSUMER CULTURAL EXPERIENCE

Advertisements have become acknowledged aspects of a widened marketing discipline within a horizontally integrated media infrastructure, and it has become difficult to see where marketing or advertising promotion stop, and PR begins. The professional distinction between communication disciplines remains, but they are overlapping with each other in practice as well as in concept. Contemporary consumer experience involves engagement with media to a degree that is historically unprecedented. Mediated communication, on TV, PC, phones, and other mobile devices, forms a part of the everyday consumer mise-en-scéne that is at the same time both intimate and pervasive. This is the context in which marketing operates, and the job of marketing professionals is to gain sensitivity to how local cultural meaning-making plays out through the experience of mediated communication. A rounded understanding of marketing has to acknowledge that it operates within a connected communication system of texts within contexts. Marketing practice, seen in terms of cultural anthropology, entails operating on an emic and also an etic level of cultural understanding.

True, there may be some conflation of different categories of communication going on here. Techniques such as product placement, sponsorship, content marketing and celebrity endorsement don't conform to a strict definition of advertising. Advertising is often defined as a paid-for promotion that has an identifiable source and a clearly communicated commercial offer. But how useful is this definition, really? From the reader's perspective, a brand is a brand, and a piece of media communication is, well, just that. Well-defined categories may be superficially convenient for an analysis of the production side of marketing, but how well do they map on to consumer experience? As a consumer, I pay attention to an advertisement if it interests me, in a given context. I treat advertising as entertainment, as do many others. Compilations of the funniest or most impressive ads regularly feature as peak time TV shows, and websites offering ads as entertainment thrive. As an interpreting consumer, there is no qualitative difference between the way I engage with an advertisement, and the way I engage with any other mediated communication that might feature a brand. I can tell the difference between media genres, of course, and I have a sense that they are supposed to cue somewhat different responses in me, the reader. But I am not compelled to behave in the way I am supposed to. I am free to feel excited and engaged by a viral video, and bored and cynical toward a paid-for spot advertisement. What is more, my cumulative experience of a brand is not internally sorted according to the different media categories I encountered. I'm a consumer, I don't care what you want to call your content. I just respond to it.

The logic of marketing practice has moved toward the notion of "content" as an abstract category for creative dramatic entertainment or information in which the brand features in some way. I am not suggesting that conventional feature advertising is redundant – this is palpably not so. I am suggesting that consumers' experiences of marketing, and our interpretive strategies for deconstructing it, are not pre-determined by the particular category of promotional communication with which we might be engaged. Advertising, sales promotion, PR, content such as sponsor's "idents" in between the show and the credits, viral videos, the mention of a brand in a radio or TV show, the sight of a logo in a post-match sports interview, or a set-piece advertising spot shown during the commercial break on TV, all form parts of a seamless stream of experience for the viewer. The communication strategies deployed in these different media channels differ, but the most powerful effects are ideological in the sense that they valorize and normalize brands and consumption in a guise that is presented not as promotion but as entertainment. The challenge for marketing practitioners is to understand the cultural contexts in which consumers encounter marketing and brands, and to find appropriate ways of configuring the various interlocking mises-en-scéne.[35]

# CHAPTER 4

# Ideologies of space

## THE MISE-EN-SCÉNE AND THE MOVING VIEWER

Packaging, product labeling, press, PR and print advertising, branded content, advertorial, Out Of Home (OOH) displays, TV and cinema advertising, viral videos, and many other media can carry marketing signs. These signs have a powerful semiotic potential that can reach deeply into our subjective experience. Our experiential worlds are populated with marketing signs as the scene props, if you will, of our lives. The mise-en-scéne analogy, though, relates to these communications in terms of the arrangement of a scene for a static viewer. The audience of the mise-en-scéne in a living room or a movie theatre usually views the scene from only one perspective, and its engagement with the scene is visual and aural, enhanced by a bit of creative imagination. The "director" of marketing may have control over just a few elements of that scene, but as Bernays calculated in his product placement initiative in New York's Easter Parade, the art lies in choosing the decisive elements, in an influential context, to achieve the desired effect.

Audiences of marketing scenes, though, are not necessarily static. They move about through marketing scenes, and thus their perspective changes. Marketing scenes include not only media scenarios that reference, show, or advertise brands, but also three dimensional walk-through or ride-through experiences. Where the viewer is physically present in the mise-en-scéne, their experience is potentially more complex and kinaesthetic that when they are viewing a mediated image. Physical presence entails using all of our senses, taking in the ambient features of a scene such as aromas, air quality, sounds, and textures. The consumers' movement through the scene presents more opportunities for marketers to try to activate emotional, cognitive, physiological, and behavioral responses. Walk-through marketing scenes could include, say, retail spaces such as banks, department stores, shopping malls, and other servicescape[1] environments such as restaurants, cinema complexes, street markets, theme parks, zoos, and other tourist attractions, hotels, sports stadia, and many more. Audiences can take in the visual experiences of the frontage of retail units or other buildings, the interior design, and the sensory experiences of the parking, queuing, eating, walking, along with the human interactions within these spaces. Add to these the pedestrianized landscape of urban shopping or nightlife areas, and you have a panoply of spaces designed with marketing in mind. Some are totally designed experiences, like theme park rides or walk-through entertainment, while others are aggregations of distinct designs, like, say, the experience of walking through the Miracle Mile shopping and eating mall off the Las Vegas strip. Still others have evolved over hundreds of years and marketing signs have been interpolated into them gradually, such as in town and city centers.

The aggregate effect created by ad hoc urban planning might collectively promote an ideology of consumerism in general rather than a particular brand, for example when you walk through streets framed with OOH advertising on billboards, animated screens, LCD displays, shop signs and posters, say, in Shinjuku or Shibuya in Tokyo, or Times Square in New York. Urban areas have their own history and architecture, and they might be dotted with urban furniture like post boxes, lamp posts, pub signs, pedestrian crossings, telephone kiosks, or Tube entrances, like Piccadilly Circus in London. Marketing intrudes into such scenes through methods that are usually contrived, and paid-for. Contemporary marketing inserts itself self-consciously into the environment, until we stop noticing its incongruity. For example, driving on British motorways through the countryside, it is now common to see

flatbed trucks parked up in lush green fields bearing advertising hoardings, as cows and sheep mill around, indifferent
to the offer. Farmers are said to earn up to £30,000 a year
in fees for road-side advertising because of the visibility and
traffic volume. Britain's green and pleasant countryside is
dotted with these highway hoardings, and the driver's eye
is irresistibly drawn to them long enough to take in the ad.
Of course, British roads are nowhere near as crowded with
advertising as in some other countries. Many urban roads in
the USA or South America, for example, are teeming with
signage and OOH hoardings. In some urban city centers,
there are so many LCD and plasma advertising displays
shrieking for attention that at night they flood the space
with a sepulchral light. This might be seen as a blight on the
landscape, but the urban rash of blinking neon in shopping
districts of Tokyo, for example, seems somehow just right, as
it does in Times Square or on the Las Vegas Strip. Curiously,
in contrast, driving up Sunset Boulevard in Hollywood, Los
Angeles, the billboard-pitted skyline seems maddening and
deranged, to me at least.

The intrusion of marketing signs into urban space is not to
everyone's taste. The idea that urban advertising amounts to
visual pollution took such a hold in Sao Paulo in Brazil that
the local authority banned advertising displays altogether in
2007. Local businesses were forced to compete by offering
such good service they'd earn publicity by word-of-mouth
referrals. Imagine! Six years on, the ban still in place, the scene
looks somewhat post-apocalyptic.[2] Out-of-home marketing
has been silenced, and hastily stripped billboards stand mute,
staring reproachfully across the indifferent city. It really isn't
an improvement.

## MARKETING INFLUENCE ON RETAIL DESIGN

There is nothing new about physical spaces being designed for
consumption, of course. Public theatres and market squares,
for example, have featured in human settlements for more

than 2000 years. But while the provision of market signs and spaces for commerce has been important throughout history, the grandest public spaces tended to be constructed for great gatherings of religious worship or communitarian public spectacle. The modern era saw commerce assuming a more eminent symbolic place as a force in architecture and urban planning. For example, historian Roland Marchand has written of the role architecture played in the legitimization of the great American corporations at the turn of the century. They constructed imposing and grandiose headquarters that bestowed an order of cultural authority on these nascent business behemoths. This helped in identifying them with the American Way, at a time when "faceless" corporations were seen by many as a threat to the American way of life because of their devastating effect on small Main Street businesses.[3] The images of these buildings were reproduced on company literature and advertising, using architecture as a PR tool. Retail emporiums quickly took up the challenge to inspire consumers with the imaginative and evocative use of physical space, for example with John Wanamaker's store in Phila-delphia, now occupied by Macy's. Paris has possibly the world's first purpose-built department store, Le Bon Marché, and the stunning La Samaritaine, a blend of art nouveau and art deco, the largest department store in Paris and home of the LMVH luxury goods brand. These cathedrals of consumption invited their guests to trade up in social class, by entering the stores, buying the goods, and acquiring the symbolic cultural capital to display in their living room, or on their arm. The semiotic force of architecture helped bring lifestyle consumption to the masses.

Today, most new retail environments operate to a different design aesthetic. They usually look more like aircraft hangars than cathedrals, and the interiors are ruthlessly functional rather than inspirational. Modern retail spaces constitute the typical consumer's three-dimensional mise-en-scène on the weekly grocery shopping expedition. They are designed to cue physiological responses, emotions, and behaviors, with the aim of promoting more consumption. Merchandising, in-store displays, sales promotion, and crowd flow and queue management in such places can be seen as inherently part of marketing in the sense that they are aspects of a co-ordinated promotional environment. Customer traffic flow is carefully calculated and funneled to generate maximum revenue, often using security camera footage to refine the model. In addition, sales promotion techniques are integrated with the spatial planning. As I write I've just returned from a trip to Marks and Spencer in the small English market town where we live (yes, I'm living the dream) and the shelves with cooled ready meals of sushi and pasta had little grab-boxes packed with brightly packaged chocolate confections attached at knee height, for toddlers to snatch and sneak into the basket. No need to ask Mum then. Perfect.

Much of our behavior in retail spaces is unreflexive, perhaps unconscious. Retailers know that if they can disable our critical faculties and engage our sensory or aesthetic response, or our emotions, we will probably spend more money. Many retail ambience-enhancing techniques are well known, such as pumping the smell of baking bread back into the store, playing muzak to lower blink-rate and lull consumers into a trance-like state, putting daily essentials at the back of the store to encourage walk-through, piling promotional deals at the entrance, and putting sweets and other impulse purchases at child's eye level. There are intense battles amongst suppliers for shelf space, since sales volume often corresponds with the footage of shelf space devoted to a brand. There is such a premium on good shelf space that major brands often have to pay major retailers to give their product more or better shelf space, or even to stock the product at all.

Years ago, *Walls* famously gave free refrigerators to shops, so they would stock their ice creams. Today, the big grocery retail chains wield oligopolistic power that enables them to dictate terms to the big brands, but they also need those brands. In turn, the retailers benefit from the cultural presence brands achieve through advertising and sponsorship. Grocery brand advertising gets people into stores, and stores compete with each other by using big brands as loss leaders. In the UK, for example, alcohol brands have achieved such cultural presence that it is now common to see them discounted in promotions, to get people through the doors. Thirty years ago this could not happen because of legal restrictions on the sale of alcohol alongside groceries, and because alcohol brands were known only to the adult drinkers who favored them. Now, alcohol brands are recognized across demographics because of intensive advertising and sponsorship. Booze brands are piled up at the entrance of the store in discount offers, just if it were any other grocery product.[4]

## URBAN SPACES AND MARKETING

Alcohol business in the UK has influenced the exterior urban landscape as well as changing the look of grocery store interiors. Since the 1980s, many urban city centers have been re-designed as drinking (sometimes called drinker-tainment) zones, with pedestrian traffic flows incorporated into the placing of venues. These zones are populated by a large number of heavily branded "vertical" drinking venues (i.e., no seats), mixed in with various branded nightclubs. Meanwhile, traditional British pubs are closing at a rapid rate. Drinking zone revelers are corralled into a manage-able few square miles. This tends to result in a lot of noise and partying at weekends, sometimes accompanied by street drinking, violence, and rowdy behavior. Many local authorities have become highly reliant on the local tax revenues from this alcohol-fuelled local economy, while residents, police, and health authorities complain that these zones create a huge and costly public nuisance through implicitly sanctioned heavy drinking. There is evidence that recent years have seen a reduction in both per capita alcohol consumption in the UK and in alcohol-related crime and street disorder, but both are declining from a historically high base and serious alcohol-related health and social problems remain in the UK.[5]

In some Las Vegas areas, the distinction between inside and outside has been designed out of the experience. The Miracle Mile shopping and eating mall has a manufactured blue cloud sky, like the one in the Jim Carrey movie *The Truman Show*. As in the movie, every now and then, the meandering shoppers get an indoor rainstorm, complete with thunder. The lighting adjusts but never quite falls into darkness – late night and early morning the mile is bathed in a warm sunset glow. Take a drive down to the low rent end of the Las Vegas Strip, Downtown, and you can find Freemont Street, a five-block area that has been roofed over with a canopy containing millions of lights. Its outside, but it isn't, you look up to the sky to see a vivid show of moving images, accompanied by music from a half-million-watt sound system. Even the real outside at the centre of the Las Vegas strip feels like a self-contained interior space because of the sensory overload of fantasy architecture, teeming crowds and neon signage. The casinos don't have clocks, and the environment is designed for people to forget about the Protestant ethos of working hours in favour of 24/7 indulgence. As an example of a marketing mise-en-scéne that disrupts our consumer ontology and bends reality to the imperative of consumption, Las Vegas is hard to beat. For some people, Vegas's brazen celebration of in-authenticity represents the apex of marketing vulgarity, and stands as a warning as to how far marketing influence can take us if we allow its control to reach too far. Personally, I rather like it, for a short holiday.

## SERVICESCAPES AND POSITIONING

Back indoors in the UK, the design and layout of drinking venues such as the chain pub franchise *Wetherspoons* is a curious melange of simulated tradition. *Wetherspoons*, like the ubiquitous global phenomenon of "Irish" themed pubs, contrives a sense of simulated authenticity by incorporating local cultural elements into pub design, decoration, and layout. In many *Wetherspoons* pubs you'll find wooden pews rather than proper seats, like the ones they'd have in medieval times, but made last week. In a few British pubs I believe you can still actually park your buttocks on the very same pews as drinkers did some 400 years ago. In *Wetherspoons* you can consume a sense of ersatz authenticity, along with your beer. Some other city-centre drinking venues eschew seating altogether, and target their offer squarely at a young, heavy-drinking market who knock back their booze raucously for a few hours from a standing position, before disappearing to the clubs. In retail environments generally, merchandising and sales techniques and interior design are carefully planned to maximize sales per square foot, and it is not only the big retail stores doing this. For example, in small CTN (Confectionary, Tobacco, Newsagent) shops there is a "golden arc" of items within the easy arm's reach of a shopper standing at the counter, and the brands that are placed within that golden arc will sell far more than those for which the customer has to move and search. Reps for the biggest brands make sure that their stock is well within that golden arc.

Some stores still use the principle of making the interior more inviting than the average punter's living room. For example, in the UK, gambling has been de-regulated in recent years and has become a major growth business. One of my sons works part-time for a major betting shop chain, and when I visited him at work I was surprised at the difference in ambience from the rough betting shops of my misspent youth. It was a luxury lounge, more comfortable and color-co-ordinated than the average British living room, with plush carpets, comfortable seating, a 4-star hotel standard of bathroom, free coffee and cola, multiple TV screens and live sports commentary. Mark you, this isn't Vegas. It's Stoke-on-Trent, a small, Northern UK city that has been in industrial decline for as long as I can recall. The walls of the lounge are lined with fixed-odds slot machines, which have been criticized for making gambling addiction far easier and more accessible. The daily revenue from these machines can be extraordinary, even in a small shop in a very small city. The comfortable ambiance of new-style "bookies" signifies the de-regulated industry's shift into mainstream consumption, with gambling taking its place alongside any other family leisure activity. In the UK, these gleaming new betting shops can often be seen in-between the scruffy fish and chip shop and the derelict pub on low-income, high-unemployment housing estates. They sit proudly as icons of decadence amidst the urban decay. My son is working his way through university and getting a rich education in life at the same time. In some shops, men come in to gamble with wives, children and push chairs left outside, eyes peering through the steamy windows, hoping there'll be some money left once Dad's need for "leisure" is sated. They don't show that in the TV adverts. Gambling in the UK is using marketing semiotics to reposition itself as a mainstream leisure pursuit, through TV advertising with high production values and (relatively) high-end store design.

Servicescapes are competitive tools. When I bought my first BMW (second hand) I was astonished at the comfort of the service area. For some 20 years I had waited for my clapped-out vehicles to be serviced in back-street garages while I sat in a freezing cold office on a wobbly chair, contemplating the fresh oil stains on my trousers, and trying not to catch the eye of the fairly hostile guy behind the counter in case he added some spurious sum to my bill for looking at him. In contrast, going into a BMW service franchise for the first time, I knew that, at last, I had arrived. The air was warm and exhaust-free, the employees smartly dressed and personable, there was no noise but soothing music, and the work schedule was well-organized. They knew who I was, and when my car would be ready. Best of all, I was treated the same way as the people who came in with cars worth ten times more than mine. The relationship management (RM) matters in a servicescape. Like most consumers, I don't really see my service providers in terms of a quasi-relationship, despite RM orthodoxy. What interests me as a consumer is interaction, in the sense of how I'm treated. I don't want my service providers to be ingratiating, and I certainly don't want a relationship, but as a consumer, I do like being treated in a friendly, polite, and ever-so-faintly flattering manner. While the intangibles of my service encounter with BMW were spot-on, the tangibles were all in place too. The plush waiting area had clean-as-a-whistle carpeting, deep leather settees, limitless free coffee or hot chocolate, biscuits, daily newspapers to read, cable TV, and, for those addicted to their email, free wifi. I've had another four second-hand BMWs since then, and one day, who knows, I might even return some of BMW's investment in free biscuits by buying a brand new one. Granted, I pay for my biscuits really – the service costs are higher than they would be if I were still servicing ten-year-old Fords at small independent garages. But I'm sold on the service. Waiting for my car to be serviced in a downtown garage used to be two hours of my life wasted. Not anymore. Oh no. Now, it's two hours sipping latte, perusing the daily news and being, well, someone else: someone a bit more important.[6]

It might seem to be stretching the notion of ideology to include commercial architecture, urban planning, in-store design and promotion or service scripts, even if we accept that they all influence our thinking and behavior in subtle ways. There are elements of environmental and economic psychology at work in service encounters. Effects are calculated: product displays, prices and lighting are adjusted, customer flow is mapped, and sales twitch as a result. Like rats in a maze, we respond unreflexively to behavioral conditioning. But spaces are seldom entirely self-contained. Like advertising, they carry inter-textual echoes of the wider world. We link in-store promotional displays and packaging with advertising and other media representations, and our buying choices, honed in-store, were already framed before we walked in. The cognitive psychology of servicescapes does not only activate entirely new behavioral responses; it also shapes the ones that have already been primed by wider cultural influences. My own encounter with BMW service, for example, is framed by my prior cultural understanding of the brand's prestige.

## MARKETING RATIONALITY PENETRATING URBAN LIFE AND CONSUMER CONSCIOUSNESS

We know, or at least we should, that stores want to sell us as much stuff as they can. These are, though, ideological spaces not only in their internal design but in the sense of the wider picture of the way the whole urban environment is subject to marketing influences through the selection and approval of planning applications, and store location, architecture, and signage. The explosion of huge retail grocery stores in developed countries has profoundly changed the way towns and cities look, and with it, the ways lives are lived. "Milk men" and "pop men," drivers who delivered milk, dairy products, and soda in the UK in the 1960s, have all but disappeared from British suburbs. The big supermarkets now sell financial services, foreign currency, electronic goods, movie DVDs, they have in-house butchers, fish mongers, you name it. Many provincial high streets are now populated mainly with charity shops and empty retail units, as customers have been sucked out of the town centers into the edge-of-town retail stores, and smaller specialist retailers have vanished. Big retail stores are convenient, the prices and quality control are usually good, and they can stock a huge range of items. The marketing offer is irresistible, but the effect on the urban landscape is palpable. Our buying habits are funneled into these corny consumer cornucopias, our spending tracked and data-mined, and our choices subtly framed. Consumers are not dupes, but we are suckers for marketing, me included.

The reach of marketing rationality into urban space is not limited to the design of retail parks. Promotion now reaches into urban spaces that formerly would have been regarded as sacred and beyond the profanity of marketing, such as churches and schools. It is well known that major drinks brands such as *Coca Cola* have contracts with schools in the USA to be the sole supplier of soda dispensing machines on campus. One child was reportedly sent home for having the audacity to wear a *Pepsi* T-shirt on his school's *Coke* promotion day. Local advertising space is sold in text books and, in some American schools, TVs have been supplied for airing educational programming, the quid pro quo being that advertising is piped directly to a lucrative, and captive, market segment: school students, while they are in their lessons. Christian churches often use advertising tropes in the signs in their grounds, or, in the USA, in their TV advertising, as they compete with Mammon to fill pews and collection plates.

We live in a culture that has absorbed marketing rationality into its very pores – a promotional culture, no less.[7] Occasionally, the tension this creates breaks the surface, but usually because of the content of an individual promotion, rather than the mere fact that it is there. In 2000, for example, outdoor posters for *Yves Saint Laurent* fragrance *Opium* featuring model Sophie Dahl dressed in a flesh-colored bodystocking, were banned after hundreds of complaints to the UK advertising regulator the Advertising Standards Authority (ASA). In 2003, billboards of women in *Sloggi* branded G-strings located outside primary schools in France sparked much angry media coverage. The intrusion into the French cityscape of *McDonald*'s restaurants was another source of cultural tension, as there were regular protests for a time and some vandalism, although *McDonald*'s is now a familiar sight in France. The *Sloggi* and *Opium* furores were good illustrations of the importance of context in the interpretation of marketing signs. The ads generated little comment when they were published as print ads in style magazines, but were viewed entirely differently when placed outside as 32-sheet OOH posters.

More recently, *Benetton* tried to reprise their heyday as the world's top-of-mind fashion brand by creating some urban disruption. In the 1990s, Olivero Toscani's photography had made an obscure Italian knitwear manufacturer the world's second most recalled brand after *Coca Cola* with photography that was more like documentary or news-footage than advertising. Toscani pushed the boundaries of advertising as a discourse form, and exposed deep contradictions in the way advertising texts are read by consumers. His posters were compelling and controversial images because as many people loved them as hated them, at least until his final, disastrous campaign featuring death row convicts. This misjudgment precipitated the end of his tenure at *Benetton* because it was the first of his campaigns to have damaging commercial implications – Sears Roebuck cancelled their in-store *Benetton* franchise as a result of the complaints. In 2012, *Benetton* showed that they never really understood what Toscani had done for them when they tried to stir up some controversial PR with "Unhate," a campaign featuring photoshopped posters of kissing heads of state and clerics. One, of the Roman Catholic Pope kissing a Turkish Imam, was unveiled on Vatican square in a crude attempt to generate PR by enraging the Vatican. Unhate's kissing figures certainly angered the Vatican but they failed abysmally to ignite a flame of public approval.[8] Toscani's most memorable images had evoked as much support as dissent, and whatever your response to the content, they were examples of striking photography. The *Unhate* images were just silly and unappealing, and although the *Unhate* theme continued to be used by *Benetton*, the kissing ads soon disappeared.

"Controversial" advertising can be useful for fashion and alcohol brands because a frisson of transgression sharpens their brand image and signifies the desired, "edgy" positioning. Brands can ingratiate themselves with young market segments by annoying older, more conservative groups, as a glance at many campaigns for *Benetton*, *Calvin Klein*, *FCUK*, *WKD* and others will attest. In the UK, TV ads are pre-vetted by a committee of the ASA, but print and OOH ads are managed on a reactive basis. As a result, they are ideal for brands that wish to ignite controversy and generate complaints, because they will get two weeks' publicity before the ASA tells them to take the ad down. So many interest groups have begun to use the idea of being offended by advertising in order to get a platform for their own publicity aims, that igniting this offence has become viable though risky marketing strategy.

The urban environment offers a convenient theatre in which OOH advertising is ideal for this ethically dubious purpose.

## MARKETING SIGNS AND CONSUMER RESISTANCE

Despite occasional public protests, ambient marketing, the insertion of promotion into the environment, typically meets little resistance. We simply take it for granted that our theatre programme, our car park ticket, or our beer mat will have advertising, and we've grown used to seeing brand logos on clothes, sports bags, sunglasses, you name it. We go outside, look up, and our eyes are regaled with billboards selling dreams. When we engage with media we expect to find it streaked with explicit or implicit marketing content. Urban city space has become just as inflected with commercial rationality as the media.

After you've considered the marketing influence built into the urban architecture, and designed into urban planning, and integrated into the interiors of retail stores, you have the less permanent marketing initiatives, the pop-up shops, the sponsored flash mobs, the fly-posters, the in-pub promotion girls, and the urban guerrillas who scrawl promotional "graffiti" on walls or set up unlicensed events, such as projecting a giant image on to the side of local landmark, only to pick up the projector and do a runner when the police arrive. I should add, before I start sounding too much like an old curmudgeon, that I do not yearn for a mythical, less commercialized world, a Britain of quiet country lanes, kindly policemen, warm beer and old maids cycling to evensong. There is still plenty of warm beer, and lots of lovely country lanes, although quite a few these days are decorated with beer cans and *McDonald*'s wrappers flung out of cars. Perhaps I am a curmudgeon after all. But the issue of marketing intruding into urban spaces is far from new. Some 400 years ago, *Punch* magazine carried irate letters from readers who were irritated and alarmed at the cacophony of promotion in London streets, from sandwich board men, leafleteers, and hucksters, to elaborately bedecked horse-drawn vehicles pronouncing on the best shops from which to buy carbolic soap. The streets were teeming with promotion and branding. Other than the technology, there isn't much that is really new in marketing. The authenticity of contemporary marketing space, though, seems somehow lacking. A Victorian shopping street with its apothecary and pub recreated in a Museum seems charming, yet when this kind of simulation is turned to a commercial purpose it seems deeply inauthentic. For newer generations, though, there is no distinction between real authenticity, however that may be conceived, and quasi-authenticity that is manufactured by marketing. Marketing signs seem to exert a cumulative ideological effect that dampens resistance. We become so used to them that we eventually see them not as marketing signs but simply as everyday features of our cultural mise-en-scéne.

## PSYCHOGEOGRAPHY AND URBAN SPACE

One example of an urban simulacrum created as a marketing enterprise is Bicester Village, in Oxfordshire, about an hour North of London. I have some familiarity with this space, having been inexplicably seduced several times by its power to make me feel more fashionable, more affluent, and more brand conscious, than I normally am. I should note, that I am naturally a bit, well, cheap, by upbringing and inclination. I'm superficial too, as you've already gathered from my pathetic capitulation to *BMW* in exchange for a free biscuit and an insincere greeting. Bicester village is a designer brand outlet that was not built for me. It was created for British fashionistas and wealthy tourists who bus down from London with crisp wads of ready cash to snap up top brands at a discount. The place was created in 1992[9] and since then, the word "boomed" hardly serves to sum up the revenues and local development that have cascaded from this shopping utopia. Bicester really is a village, with a long and distinguished place in old Oxfordshire history, but Bicester brand outlet "village" is not in the real Bicester Village. It is sited on the real village's outside edge. Bicester outlet village is a made-up village high street, immaculately paved, spotlessly clean, and lined with more than 100 solid-looking shops, all selling the biggest global brands of clothing and accessories.

As I move through this postmodern mise-en-scéne it puts me in mind of psychogeographical writing. One flâneurs along, taking in the pleasing pseudo-urban ambience, feeling at one with marketing, and submitting to the invisible thread that pulls one into the shops. The lack of resistance in Bicester Village is its most striking feature. Somehow, one gives oneself up willingly to the ideology of the brand, merely by entering the space. At least I do. The literary genre of psychogeography explores the psychological and emotional effects of the urban environment, and entails a critique, as well as an appreciation. Psychogeography embraces contrast, conflict, and contradiction, and highlights the personal, subjective perspective. It appeals to me because of its focus on the experience of moving through urban spaces, while also trying to be aware of one's responses to them. It is better known as a literary genre than as a critical discipline, in work by such authors as Daniel Defoe, Thomas De Quincey, Robert Louis Stevenson, Edgar Allen Poe, and William Blake, although it has been invoked as a method of political critique by Guy Debord and the revolutionary Situationist International.[10] Debord took Walter Benjamin's concept of the flâneur, the perceptive but critical urban wanderer, as the basis for his technique of détournement. Détournement involved creating urban "situations" designed to subvert capitalism. Contemporary equivalents might include subvertising, or "culture jamming" techniques, such as parodying advertisements or defacing billboards with wittily subversive amendments. For Debord, capitalism consisted of a "Spectacle" of mediated imagery of entertainment and consumption which destroyed our ability to respond emotionally to our environment. He argued that a sense of the authenticity of lived experience had to be reclaimed through subversion of urban spaces. This often meant some kind of drunken riot. Debord's idea of the Spectacle seemed to refer largely to the role of mediated imagery, especially advertising, in promoting capitalistic propaganda in the form of lifestyle images of blissful consumption. Henri Lefebvre, on the other hand, who was for a time a collaborator of Debord's, focused more on the spatial elements of capitalism rather than its mediated imagery, and wrote of the "ideologies of space" as the influence urban planning, architecture, and design exerts on human subjectivity. Urban spaces, he suggested, are far from neutral but are invested with ideologies that influence the way subjectivities, relationships and behavior are constituted within them.

Modern writers like J.G. Ballard and Will Self have also taken up the psychogeographical theme. One might add to the canon of pyschogeography, if it isn't stretching the genre category too far beyond Gothic London and Paris, writers such as Jack Kerouac, Cormac McCarthy, Anthony Burgess (for *A Clockwork Orange*), and a personal favorite of mine, an old David Lynch movie called *Eraserhead*. In another example, the movie of John O'Brien's novel *Leaving Las Vegas*, with actor Nicholas Cage, is an example that poignantly evinces the dark underbelly lurking beneath many psychogeographical narratives, set against one of the world's most evocative urban mises-en-scéne. In psychogeographical narrative there is a sense that the urban and the psychological are intimately connected, usually in a bad way. The characters move uneasily through a darkened landscape that is potent with threat, and they explore their own collapsing psyches in juxtaposition with the decay of their environment. When crisis hits, it is sudden, and violent, as in, say, Ballard's dystopian visions of urban violence and sexual depravity.

All of which, might put you more in mind of a Saturday morning visit to the local *Tesco*, rather than a stroll through the urban fiction of Bicester brand outlet "village." One of the most compelling aspects of the Bicester village mise-en-scéne is the steely calmness it bestows on its visitors as they roam the space applying their discernment, as if mentally weighing the symbolic cultural capital to be earned from paying £35 (down from £60) for a *Polo* T-shirt. Everything is relative when a £400 jacket, reduced from £2,800, looks like a bargain. When you make your way from the vast car parks, which are veritable open air showrooms of luxury motor cars, the first thing you notice is the cleanliness of the neatly paved pedestrian area. Not so much a chewing gum wrapper blights the walkways. The next thing I notice is the emotional containment. There is a Bicester manner that the shop staff have off to a tee, urbane, tidily presented, discrete, slightly aloof, but very nice and approachable. The manner extends to most of the visitors, although I admit I never go during the weekend when there are queues snaking out of each smartly appointed store, with hoards of consumers penned into roped-off walkways by shop bouncers, as if they're waiting for admission to the VIP lounge of a nightclub. A lot of visitors seem to go there to be part of the Spectacle, to look and to be seen. There are rich Daddy's girls, arms hung with lines of beautifully embossed designer shopping bags, shady-looking but elegantly dressed men in expensive overcoats, expensive-looking middle-aged ladies on a girl's day out, wealthy foreign families sharing a shopping and wealth-flaunting experience, along with a few flashy track-suited yokels and sweating tourists. And me. It's worth going just for the people-watching.

The effect is subtle, even though the artifice is anything but. It is a street that is not a street. For one thing, there are no Oxfam charity shops, tattoo parlors, pubs, or Chinese take-aways, no smell of diesel fumes, no traffic noise, no litter, no raucous shouting. There are two or three smart but informal cafes, but the rest of the units are immaculately presented small "boutiques" offering *Amorino*, *Annoushka*, *Armani*, and every other prestige style brand in the alphabet. The streets are carefully policed and there are no *Big Issue* sellers or loitering hoodie gangs. I imagine crime is common there, but I've never seen any. The crowd is generally expensive-looking, poised, polite, multi-cultural, and with a slightly dissociated air, with everyone fixed on a common purpose- acquiring brands. My kids had never seen so many clean, smartly dressed people in a shopping area before. The smartness and cleanliness of the crowds lends an air of unreality to the place, so radical is the contrast with a typical British city centre.

The contradictions of this ersatz world are striking. It is a riot of self-indulgence, yet with none of the exuberance one might expect. The ambience is emotionally contained, despite occasional outbursts of unseemly scrabbling at the most heavily discounted displays. Just now and then there appears a cultural rift between foreign shoppers who expect service with a capital S, and retail staff who expect to be treated as equals. The egalitarian spirit of brand camaraderie usually obtains, maintaining the sheen of social harmony. It is a festival of ostentation, yet also a theatre of thrift. Everyone is seeking high fashion brands, but at a discount. The tight-fistedness of the wealthy is legendary, but part of Bicester's psychogeographical effect seems to be that parsimony is publicly paraded as an extension of one's brand discernment. Penny-pinching is ok if you're a member of the brand cognoscenti. Yet another contradiction is that to experience Bicester's brand-topia is to go on a quest for personal authenticity, yet in a wholly inauthentic setting. But, I ask myself, "is not there a tinge of subversion about this very street with its rejection of grimy reality, its insistence on the cultural distinction of brand style, and its symbolic social mobility?" The world of brands is where, in the right company, the ownership and display of a bag or a suit can do more to elevate your social standing than the overwrought social policy of earnest politicians. It is the realization of the proletarian dream – class is dissolved, replaced by a mere object that is within the reach of anyone with a credit card. Class distinction collapses into the symbolism of a watch or a shirt.

True, there are some teeny weeny problems with brand democracy. One is that, if your social status is maintained with symbols, you may never have enough. I get the sense that many of the brand cognoscenti are symbol junkies. A branded item might be the entry ticket to a social group, but once inside, jockeying for position in the hierarchy of brand cultural capital becomes a daily source of tension. In some universities around the world, for example, there is a social group for the girls with the right branded bag, another for those with the good fake branded bag, and still another for the girls with the really cheap fake bag. They can call a fake branded item with a momentary glance, and social prospects for the next four years, and beyond, can be defined in that one, appraising glance. British school playgrounds, unfortunately, are another site in which the brand is often used as a proxy for the person. Kids have to have the right brand to be in the cool gang. My own fascination with Bicester comes from the way, once in the street, I am drawn into the belief that I, too, actually need a pair of £160 *Hugo Boss* shoes (down from £250). Clearly, a lot of the visitors don't need much persuading. This typically British "village," except it isn't, throngs with South East Asian and Middle Eastern consumers who are making substantial savings on the prices back home, for stuff they hardly need. The handbag shops display the products like museum artefacts, on a plinth, with a price tag of hundreds, or thousands, for a bag big enough for car keys and a packet of *Handy Andies*. The teeming plastic street of Bicester village is the quintessence of hyper-reality; it is a living advertising scene, where there is no grimy reality to break through the shiny surface of brand heaven.[11]

Admittedly, Bicester is not a part of the real urban landscape. It's a simulacrum of an urban scene, a fantasy of moulded plastic. It isn't Corso Vittorio Emanuele in Milan, Rodeo Drive in Beverly Hills, or even Oxford Street. It's both less, and more. It's the face of elegant shopping, but without any unsightly urban warts. There are no dog faeces, there's no construction work, no noise, no beggars, and no potholes. There are, instead, clean, modern toilet facilities, convenient bench seats complete with soft cushions and blankets, arty street ornaments, and food outlets serving crepes and luxury ice cream. In-keeping with the mise-en-scéne spirit, there is no sense of pressurised selling, and no hurry. The viewer can wander at leisure through the scene, taking in the sensory experience, and deciding for him or herself what response, if any, is due. You can go for a day trip, enjoy the window shopping and buy nothing at all. What Bicester shares with other, real, legendary shopping streets is a concatenation of luxury brand boutiques, unhindered walkways, easy access to shop fronts, and an ambience which ideologically supports extravagant expenditure as an exercise in the acquisition of cultural capital. Its persuasive force is semiotic, not coercive.

## THE URBAN MARKETING SPECTACLE

Bicester Village, though, is an easy example of a marketing space that elicits an emotional investment from the consumer. Perhaps less obvious to most of us is the ideological element of those urban spaces we take for granted because they have been the setting of our lives, like city centers, inner-city industrial areas, or suburban housing estates. Guy Debord's revolutionary ideas produced no revolution, and his methods yielded little social scientific work. However, his notion of a Spectacle of marketing and consumption that obliterates authentic life and replaces it with a pale imitation based on passive consumption, retains its force. Debord's Spectacle of marketing, advertising, and violent and sexualized entertainment blunts the response to environment. For Debord, consumers under capitalism live in a shadow world that is defined by capital. Consumers lose the ability to realize our senses of individuality and authenticity without recourse to the values, symbols, and tools provided for us, by marketing. For Merlin Coverley,[12] psychogeography refers to our reliance on (commercially inflected) mediated images, as a result of which we lose our ability to achieve cathartic joy through a sensory engagement with our environment. The eventual consequence is the psychological, and social, implosion of which Ballard and McCarthy write. Whether or not one finds Debord's ideas plausible, they offer a compellingly bleak account of the psychological effects of our marketing environment.

Perhaps an analogy with Debord's Spectacle might be seen in the drinkertainment zones I mentioned earlier, the city-centre pedestrian areas planned for easy staggering from bar to bar. Not only the drinks but the drinking venues are branded experiences that activate the upper layers of advertising, promotion, and sponsorship. But these zones are not like Bicester Village, where the passivity before the Spectacle is palpable. They are also spaces for the subversion of the Spectacle in the form of the happy, relaxed "sensible" drinking promoted by government and alcohol marketing and advertising. There is drunkeness, fighting, public urination, vomiting, and other forms of Rabelasian excess. Drinking in these areas passively serves the Spectacle of alcohol marketing, and the wild excesses subvert it, as if the madness of alienation brought about by the Spectacle might be exorcised through an insane excess of violent consumption. The UK government has used the plea to "drink sensibly" in countless public pronouncements and policy documents on the UK's alcohol problems.[13] No term could serve better to inflame the transgressive urge to drink in a spirit of carniva-lesque excess, in a rich parody of the Spectacle of "sensible" consumption. Saturday night in many British city centers is the very antithesis of calm, Bicesterine consumption. Guy Debord would have approved.

## CONTEXT AND CULTURAL CRITIQUE

My logic, here, is that if urban spaces, including architecture, planning, street furniture, signage, shop frontage, and interior design, are ideologically linked to capitalism, that is, if they are inflected with the values of marketing, then this insight should be at the very centre of marketing study and practice. The place of cultural critique is not at the sniping periphery of academic critical theory, but at the centre of a candid and inclusive appraisal of contemporary marketing. True, urban design is not generally under the control afforded to the architects of Bicester Village or the designers of visitor experiences at Disneyland, Alton Towers, or Universal Studios. Real cities evolve as the products of many competing interests, and do not succumb to a simplistic, totalizing logic. That is their fascination. However, there is connection between my experience of rummaging the cheap shelf at Bicester *Ralph Lauren*, that of my fellow shoppers, and the wider environment that frames our sense of meaning. The fact that Bicester is so successful tells us something not only about the eternal desire for a bargain, but of the cultural landscape in which paying £400 for a jacket can be seen as a steal. In an era of economic crisis, a visit to Bicester any day of the week shows that there is still a lot of money around to spend on fun, and not just by tourists.

Much of marketing focuses resolutely on the micro instead of the macro. The cognitive psychology of buying decisions is often conceived as if our cognitions occur in a cultural vacuum. This is no more true of our interpretation of the meaning of an advertisement, than it is of our interpretation of, and response to, our physical and spatial environment. For example, I have touched on the role of alcohol and drunkenness in UK policy debates. The ways we drink, though, are cultural constructions. Research suggests that the way people behave when drunk is culturally primed more than chemically determined. In the UK, being drunk is often associated with the transgression of social norms, and especially with violence that is seemingly out-of-control. Yet, the way we drink, and the ways we behave when drunk, vary greatly amongst different cultural and ethnic groups. Societies that report greater alcohol problems are not necessarily those with higher overall consumption levels or lower abstinence rates. Even when drunk, behavior is culturally constructed according to internalized norms and cultural predispositions.

This book is about trying to understand marketing practice, techniques, and effects. It isn't a cultural critique, but I feel that cultural critique is implied, and made possible, through a more candid appreciation of the cultural marketing mise-en-scéne. Critical psychogeography is useful for conceptualizing the dynamism of environmental influence in marketing. It enriches the mise-en-scéne metaphor with sense of the way the urban environment psychologically influences moving crowds. Bicester Village has generated jobs, income and development on a considerable scale. No doubt, residents have differing views on whether that has been positive, or negative, for the area. Some critics might take the view that the Bicester experience reflects the cultural poverty of marketing's contribution to society. The fascination, to me, is to look at the cultural dynamic of how such an extraordinary phenomenon comes to pass.

## MARKETING AND GENEROSITY

As part of a balanced cultural critique it makes sense to acknowledge the elements of marketing mises-en-scéne that are well-designed with the enjoyment and comfort of the consumer in mind. As a servicescape, Bicester demonstrates a pretty good understanding of what makes a congenial buying environment for visitors. It provides a comfortable and culturally coherent context for brand shopping- there isn't a *McDonald*'s, the food outlets offer tasty European and Asian style snacks. The facilities are clean, convenient and well-decorated, the ambience is calm, the security and service efficient and discrete. The experience is designed with cultural capital in mind, yet there is none to be gained from the location. Shopping for one's designer wear in the iconic boutiques of Paris or Milan is the genuine experience, of which Bicester is a faint, slightly cheaper copy. But, like the great department stores, it invests consumption with social aspiration. What Bicester shares with "content" marketing is an open textured character that invites a semiotic engagement. The offer, the experience, is given away. It's a generous invitation to enjoy prime window shopping, people watching, and open air strolling in a safe, clean, and colorful environment. Car parking access is easy and free of charge. Just as one might enjoy some marketing content in the form of a YouTube video, Bicester Village is a gift to urban flâneurs without the fortitude to venture into edgier city spaces, or the funds to stroll in the couture capitals of Europe.

Consumer mises-en-scéne such as Bicester leave generous room for the consumers to apply their own interpretive strategies. The space for interpretation creates a vacuum that draws engagement. It is, if you will, a freemium model, and generosity, an under-recognized virtue in marketing, can be reciprocal. Consumers pick up the implication that generous expenditure reflects the power and magnanimity of the spirit. We like to be worthy of such environments as Las Vegas, Bicester, or Rodeo Drive, if we have the means. Many of us like to feel generous, and we like to reciprocate in response to social cues. Spending a large sum of money on oneself may not be the kind of generosity that will bring an egalitarian utopia to the world, but it should not be dismissed as a consumer cultural motive. Generosity that benefits oneself and entails no real sacrifice may be seen as a form of self-aggrandisement, but then motives are seldom undiluted by self-interest.

The opposite is also true – parsimony begets a similar response. In some hotels, for example, much that you'd expect to be included in the price turns out to be extra, with two levels of tax and a heavily cued 20% tipping expectation on top. This can leave you feeling chiseled if the service is anything less than top notch. Where the wifi, gym and pool, breakfast, newspaper and in-room water are included, guests are more likely to upgrade the room and take meals at the hotel restaurant. Hotels that make people feel welcome tend to do better in the long run. Ladders of hidden charges may help marketers to advertise a low basic rate, but consumers soon become resentful when this low price turns out to be a fiction. Generosity in marketing offers, in contrast, tap into our instincts around reciprocal gift giving, if the circumstances, and the consumers, are right. Anthropologists have noted that giving with unconditional generosity signified high social status in some pre-industrial societies that practiced potlatch.[14] Giving generously can signify cultural leadership.

I don't claim that a bid for cultural leadership formed part of the articulated strategy behind Bicester Village, and neither would I suggest that it is advisable for all marketers to ignore pricing and revenue and give stuff away free of charge instead. Rather, the reciprocity, the exchange of value, that is central to marketing is more clearly communicated and understood in some offers than others. Consumers like to feel that they are getting value, and we like to feel that our custom is wanted and appreciated. Marketing can be more than a mere transaction in which each party is intent on minimizing outlay and maximizing utility. It can be conceived as a symbolic communication.

A deeper understanding of marketing requires a sense of how ideological influence plays through communication and the physical environment. There is also a need to understand the symbolic exchange that occurs in marketing processes. This is not a call for marketing to be re-cast as cultural geography, in which there are many academic studies of consumption and space.[15] Rather, the point indicates the intimate connection between the most astute marketing practice and the lived experience of consumers. Contextual thinking in marketing is fluid and connected, and it entails a consideration of dimensions of marketing influence that fall beyond the typical demarcations of the discipline. Practitioners do not need an academic anthropologist's grasp of the significance of gift-giving or the symbolism of objects[16] nor do they need a cultural geographer's theorization of the way spaces intersect subjectivities. What marketers do need is a wider notion of what marketing means and how it can be crafted to engage with consumer cultural experience.

# CHAPTER 5

# Marketing Ideology and Social Policy

## MARKETING IDEOLOGY IN COURSES AND BOOKS

Before leaving the topic of ideology in marketing, I want to mention one other source, in addition to ideologies of media communication, and ideologies of space. Marketing is itself a source of ideology, through its conventional axioms, concepts, and values, conveyed via mainstream text books and courses. The reason this is relevant here is that, before trying to engage with strategies for putting contextual marketing into practice, some myths about marketing need to be exposed. Many of the problems with marketing implementation arise because of misconceptions about what it is and what it can accomplish, and the major source of these misconceptions is marketing itself. Business schools are especially culpable in cleaving to a formulaic notion of marketing that suits the commodification of higher education and seems to fit with a wider neo-liberal agenda, but fails to articulate the particularities of practice. The educational route to a marketing career entails a good deal of learning that has to be unlearned once practice is encountered.

Marketing has become closely identified with particular ways of conceptualizing and talking about markets and management. Getting past the loose terminology around what marketing is and what it can do is a difficult task of organizational politics for anyone who wants to engage in contextual marketing. The fault for the cardboard cut-out version of marketing that dominates discourses about the subject, lies squarely with marketing itself. There is a set of popular ideas and conventions for talking and thinking about marketing, and these have been reproduced and reified in taught courses, academic research programmes, text books, and consultancy. Marketing has a set of normative axioms rather than scientific principles, and these tend to be placed beyond question since managerial marketing studies, generally, lacks a sense of critical self-analysis. Marketing discourse is known for its how-to, can-do tone, its relentlessly positive spin and its narcissistic blind spot toward its own intellectual contradictions. The marketing concept dictates that satisfying consumer needs and wants is the be-all and end-all of marketing, and the Marketing Mix lists the demand management tools available to marketers for carrying this out. Marketing that departs from these tenets doesn't really fit the stereotypical mould. Yet, as I've tried to illustrate with many examples, much of the most interesting marketing innovation springs from creative cultural leadership, and not from a mechanistic process of organized need satisfaction. What is more, in practice few marketing professionals enjoy control over the Mix elements of price, product design, distribution channel, and promotion. These are often dictated by other departments, by available resources, or by competitive conditions. Marketing practitioners seldom enjoy the status of directors of the mise-en-scéne. In many cases they are set dressers or prop managers. The ideological concept of market orientation implies a co-ordinated, cross-organizational effort, but marketing tasks are often broken down by functional barriers or practical considerations. In any case, the idea of need satisfaction itself is an ideological tool of legitimation for marketing. Marketing's overall purpose, obviously, is not to satisfy needs and wants, but to create them.

Consumption drives economic development and growth, and marketing serves growth not by pandering to consumer whim, but by framing consumption choices within an overarching culture of consumption. To be sure, there is a utilitarian element to marketing, and customers like to feel that we get value for our money. Marketing helps to solve consumer problems, and it drives costs down. The real terms cost of many items in the UK is lower than 30 years ago, and electronic gadgets, TVs, and microwaves are common in the households of every demographic. But our senses of value and utility are themselves culturally constructed. What we conceive as good value is relative: as consumers we do not measure utility against an absolute standard. A contextual approach to marketing is required to conceptualize its culturally constructed character and to account for the role of marketing in the lived experience of consumers. We grasp at the symbols of marketing to distract us from our lives, our social position, our tedium, our mortality. Marketing can transform mundane consumption into something rich in social symbolism. We like buying stuff, it is fun, and it turns the wheels of commerce. My point is that need satisfaction is pretty low on the consumer marketing agenda, yet is it repeated as an ideological motif in countless discourses of marketing. Marketing ideology serves a purpose, sustaining books, courses, organizational and political agenda, but it clearly limits the ways marketing can be conceived and relegates critical thinking about marketing to the fringes of the discipline.

On the other hand, leaving critique of marketing to other humanities or social science subjects will not do. A critical intellectual take on marketing can be found in literary and cultural studies and sociology, but while these may be theoretically more sophisticated than marketing studies, they suffer from a lack of understanding of marketing practice. In sociological terms, they lack a sense of the material practices of the field. Academic sociology focusing on marketing and consumption can be naive about how marketing "works"[1] and often lacks a sense of the history and practices of the field. Academics engaged in critique of marketing can unwittingly reproduce marketing's own hyperbolic claims about its own power. Anti-marketing arguments can thus become as ideologically spun as pro-marketing arguments.

Marketing operates within intersecting cultural fields; it is not set apart from other influences, such as family, ethnicity, religion, class, and economy. Seen broadly as a catch-all label for promotional and selling activity, marketing is but one element of our cultural field. There is, I believe, plenty of scope for consumer resistance, dissent, and non-compliance, and many incidents of managerial marketing success that can be attributed to cock-ups, accidents, and mistakes. Powerful as it can be, marketing is a very long way from achieving the degree of consumer control it sometimes claims, and to which many commercial interests would aspire. It holds a conflicted role as a field identified with social exchange, but also with manipulation and exploitation. It is regarded with suspicion for what is seen as its sinister sophistication as a dark art that creates all manner of social ills, yet it is also widely derided for the vacuity of its ideas and techniques. As a result of these contradictions, within organizations as well as in wider society, marketing faces a constant need to legitimize itself.

There are, then, strains of ideology that run through the common ways in which marketing and advertising are conceived and talked about. Particular genres of management writing are, in themselves, inflected with ideology.[2] I'm again referring to ideology not in the sense of party political or religious beliefs, but in a looser sense as sets of ideas that are represented as taken-for-granted or self-evident, but which in fact are based on a particular world-view and uphold narrow interests that are presented as beyond dispute. Marketing studies, as a genre of text book and how-to management publishing, is often mocked for its simplistic axioms and hyperbolic tone. Much writing in the field closes down self-critique in favour of a neutral and mechanistic idea of marketing that purportedly serves universal interests. One rarely finds discussions of art and aesthetics, critical semiotics, rhetoric,[3] or representation in a typical educational course or introductory textbook on marketing, even though those topics can yield extremely useful insights into marketing's effects. Indeed, many expert practitioners in advertising and branding draw on an intellectual background in those fields. Marketing practice seems, at times, sharply at odds with business school discourse in the way that the former embraces an eclectic range of liberal arts intellectual backgrounds at the highest levels. I feel that marketing education in university courses adds most value to students' experience if it is taught as a critical and liberal discipline, rather than a mechanistic and ethically neutral one.[4] Yet, marketing's most popular forms of literary representation tend to eschew a more penetrating examination of its effects by ruling them beyond the legitimate scope of inquiry. The difficulty this presents for marketing management is that effective contextual marketing may not fit the typical simplistic stereotype of marketing practice. Innovative marketing professionals with creative ideas for contextual marketing applications have the additional difficulty of challenging others' preconceptions about marketing.

One can understand that the marketing text book publishing industry is keen to stick to a winning formula. The short sentences, lack of meaningful integration with wider social scientific and humanities literatures, and technical vocabulary of typical text books have become a taken-for-granted aspect of the genre. Indeed, part of the popularity of marketing as a discourse can be attributed to its techniques of literary representation with its short, punchy axioms, alliterative acronyms, and case-based narrative. The effect, though, has been to make popular taught courses in marketing studies linguistically and conceptually less demanding than other social science and humanities subjects, at least at an intro-ductory level. The bite-sized topics and four-color printing of the best-selling marketing text books may be packed with entertaining case vignettes, but they're compiled in an encyclo-pedic style without extended narrative argument. I haven't used these books in my own teaching for 15 years, but they remain mainstays of a great many marketing courses. They are not without value. There is an argument that fact- and case-cramming have value as a preparation for management training. Commercial reasoning cannot be developed without knowledge of the facts of business, and marketing courses have a role in helping accelerate this descriptive learning for students who lack the necessary breadth of knowledge about business and management. Nonetheless, few would deny that extended theoretical analysis, can, when combined with experience, have a powerful effect on judgment, and training in judgment, in the end, is what university education in the humanities and social sciences offers.

University politics is not confined to marketing and management studies. There are battles over curricula content in every subject. Business studies is unique because of its sheer scale as a pedagogic enterprise. The ideological divisions within it operate in independent silos. The dominant model is a simplistic classroom approach married to an over-scientised research enterprise. A far smaller number of courses and research studies adopt a liberal and critical intellectual basis in teaching and research. You could say that typical marketing courses marry a "hard," physical science view of research to a mechanistic but anecdotal model of practice. On the other side of the pedagogic divide, other courses in marketing and consumer research adopt a liberal arts model that incorporates critique and takes a more theoretically informed approach. This reflects a real schism in the way marketing is conceived, taught, and written about in universities.

The divide is ideological, in the sense that many university business schools see their role as being pro-business, and this means that teaching and research approaches to marketing that embrace cultural critique are sometimes viewed with deep suspicion. At worst, they can be assumed to reflect a Marxist antipathy toward all capitalism. In many American university business schools, for example, an academic who departs from the uncritical, technical, pro-business ideology, will be most unlikely to win tenure. The ideological tone of marketing studies is thus institutionalized in the very place where the knowledge is produced: universities. For many managers, marketing and the other management disciplines are out of touch with practice, and our books and research projects are of interest only to other groups of like-minded academics. If academic marketing is to reach out to engage more meaningfully with policy and practice it needs to acknowledge its ideological narrowness and open up to a wider range of intellectual perspectives. Marketing, to me, is fun and fascinating, and far too important not to take seriously as a topic that demands a critical engagement informed by critical humanities and social science perspectives. My fortunate professional role is to try to say something about it that might be interesting, and possibly even useful, to students, practitioners, policy makers, and others who are, like me, interested for curiosity's sake in understanding more of its mysterious ways. A fuller understanding of marketing would be a positive thing for everyone who has a stake in it, which is everyone. The ideological character of the university approach to marketing study and research is not only of interest as a matter of internal university politics. It has proved hugely influential in the way marketing is conceived in the wider world.

## SOCIAL MARKETING AND "NUDGE" THEORY AS POLICY TECHNIQUES

There are several cases of government policy that highlight the way marketing is sometimes used in an uncritical, ideologically tainted way. I mentioned at the beginning of the book that "behavioral economics" has become a much talked-about and, seemingly, influential tool of state in recent years. Also called "nudge theory," behavioral economics refers to a pragmatic and atheoretical approach to the modification of the behavior of citizens, often based on evidence from randomized control trials. The idea is to change behavior in incremental ways without the expense or process of legislation. It has been credited with some successes. For example, one story suggested that the discipline was responsible for increasing the rate at which parking fines were paid simply by re-phrasing the letters sent to miscreants informing them of the parking violation.[5] Nudge theory nudges behavior in a direction that is assumed to be beneficial for all and benign for the individual, often by using subtle cognitive cues. Of course, this is exactly what many marketing techniques do, but the term "marketing" has become associated with big budget promotions and private sector influence, so the new hybrid discipline of "nudge" seems to have fitted more neatly into policy agenda. Nudge theory claims intellectual roots in behaviorism and economics. As the unplanned child of two disciplines with very uneven records of achievement, it is surprising that it has assumed an influential place at the high table of policy. It is regarded as controversial because of the way it circumvents the democratic legislative process to influence citizens' behaviors. Its interventions normally cost little public money, but some are worried about the implications for democracy. Marketing, ostensibly the definitive discipline of consumer persuasion, has ceded authority in policy matters to an imposter because its lack of self-critique has stunted its development. Yet, despite its lack of credibility, marketing campaigns still attract huge budgets to push policy agenda.

Oddly, government marketing campaigns that purport to promote better citizenship seem to attract less public criticism than nudge initiatives, even though they cost a fortune and deliver dubious results. Marketing ideology has taken hold in every quarter of public, private, non-profit, professional services, and charitable activity. It has crept into politics, and then into government itself. Today, marketing ideology is profoundly influential in framing large sums of taxpayer-funded marketing campaigns. By "government marketing campaigns" I am referring to public safety, civic duty, and health promotion campaigns, rather than party political marketing. Political advertising and marketing has become widely used and normalized in UK politics, following the American model, since the 1990s.[6] Political marketing, though, is funded by the parties themselves, and not by the taxpayer. By "government marketing" I mean state-funded marketing campaigns, commissioned by the incumbent government, that are presented as politically neutral and non-partisan, but socially beneficial. For some years in the UK, under the Labour Government, the Central Office of Information (COI) was the single largest buyer of advertising in the UK. Campaigns encouraged citizens to do such things as give up smoking, to drive more safely, to eat more healthily, or to vote, and tried to dissuade them from doing uncitizenly things like defrauding state benefits, taking illegal drugs, or getting excessively drunk. The newly elected coalition government abolished the COI on assuming office in 2010, and cancelled the annual government advertising budget of around half a billion pounds sterling,[7] to the distress of the advertising industry. However, in 2011, the coalition government began once again to allocate budget to government-produced advertising. They had been presented with evidence that the cessation of advertising has caused a precipitous drop in the number of people accessing government websites and telephone help-lines for quitting smoking and other healthy living advice. Smoking and poor diet cause a huge drain on public funds in costs to the UK National Health Service treating preventable diseases, so the cost of an advertising campaign, even when it amounts to scores of millions of pounds, can seem relatively good value. The logic of this is cemented by the tactic employed by health lobbies of putting a putative economic cost on unhealthy habits – the cost to the UK of excessive alcohol consumption has been estimated at £20 billion per year.[8] These figures are bandied about with a quite spurious air of precision, when they are at best hypothetical. Nonetheless, spending a few million on a high profile campaign to address the problem seems, by comparison, a good use of taxpayers' money.

Socially responsible marketing, called social marketing for short, means marketing for good causes, usually but not necessarily non-commercial ones. Governments like it. The argument is, if marketing is so powerful at shaping the behavior of citizens in bad ways, by encouraging them to smoke, drink, eat junk food, gamble, drive too fast, get into debt, and other self-indulgent vices, then why shouldn't it be used to encourage socially positive behaviors, like safer driving, "sensible" drinking, eating more healthily, and giving up smoking? The "why-should-the-Devil-have-all-the-best-tunes?" logic seems plausible enough. Fight fire with fire, and all that.

The argument is also used, with reverse logic, to justify restrictions in marketing. For example, cigarette advertising on British television was banned in 1965, with all forms of cigarette advertising being banned in 2003. In 2013, Australia banned cigarette branding on packs, and there have been successive rafts of restrictions in between. In the UK, advertising of foods that are high in fat, sugar, and salt (known as HFSS foods) has been banned on children's television, and the doctor's union, the British Medical Association, has been calling for a ban on alcohol advertising for several years. The logic of using social marketing as an arm of policy seems clear. No one can control every element of the consumer mise-en-scéne, not even global corporations or the State, but a judiciously crafted and carefully placed marketing intervention might just elicit the desired audience response. Social marketing, like behavioral economics, is credited with the power to elicit voluntary compliance to the wishes of the State. If that phrase sounds a little loaded, I mean it to indicate the worries some people have expressed about the state-sponsored use of techniques of behavioral influence other than legislation or political speeches. It also raises the issue that these techniques are not only useful for enlisting the compliance of citizens in state objectives: they are also useful for presenting those objectives as if they are in the interests of everyone. Setting aside concerns about democratic process, it seems to me that there is less disquiet amongst citizens about the use, by the state, of behavioral influence through social marketing, than there is about the use of behavioral economics.

As ever, though, it is easy to forget that there are many socio-cultural layers to the marketing context. As we saw earlier in the book, cigarette smoking, for example, didn't become popular only through advertising. It became popular because of a far wider complex of socio-cultural currents, along with the cultural valorization of smoking in movies and, through Edward Bernays, in news media. I wouldn't say this exactly supports Big Tobacco's claims that marketing causes only brand switching and doesn't increase overall demand. The valorization and legitimacy of smoking, like any other consumption practice, has to be renewed, refreshed and supported, and advertising no doubt played its role. But advertising is just one element of the consumer mise-en-scéne. In the UK, about 20% of adults smoke cigarettes today, half the figure of 20 years ago, but this is not just because of restrictions on marketing. These have been supported with legislation against smoking in public places, tax rises on cigarettes, and blanket media coverage about the harm to health. The marketing restrictions were part of a much wider awakening to the real damage caused by smoking, and, all together, the value of smoking as a social currency, signifying sophistication, urbanity, and power, was eroded. In fact, it's gone into reverse: smoking cigarettes now signifies a deficit of cultural capital, rather than a surfeit of it. The incidence of smoking is now highest among poorer and less educated demographics. The reduction in rates of cigarette smoking is often held up as a success of social policy that was achieved partly through government anti-smoking publicity campaigns and legislation, but the effects were also contingent on the wider cultural context.

## THE LIMITS OF ADVERTISING BANS

Within the marketing industry, advertising bans, in themselves, are thought to be weak measures. One example can be seen in the UK's child obesity problem. The TV ban on HFSS food advertising during children's programming seems to have yielded little effect on the booming obesity rates amongst the UK's children, about a third of whom are now reported to be overweight. Some health and medical groups are now calling for a wider-ranging ban[9] on all HFSS food advertising throughout all media. The ban on advertising "junk" food to kids seemed a good idea to many people at the time. Advertising is often in the first line of criticism as a putative cause of social harm, since it is visible every day, and, on the face of it, it is easy for governments to control. No one has the power to shut down fast food outlets, so cutting off the demand by cutting advertising seems a more plausible strategy. Of course, this oversimplifies advertising effects, and it turned out that banning HFSS advertising to children was more complex than it initially seemed. Defining HFSS foods is not unproblematic because the category includes ostensibly good foods like cheese and olive oil. Defining children's TV programming wasn't so easy either. In the UK, much TV that is not made specifically for children attracts young viewers, such as soap operas, and talent and game shows. What is more, children are watching less TV and spending more time on the internet, where there are few restrictions on promotion. Besides, junk food has become culturally normalized and has a ubiquitous retail presence in many towns and cities. If television advertising is not the dominant influence on children's eating habits, then a TV advertising ban on HFSS foods would have little effect.

Particular advertisements can resonate powerfully with young people, but TV advertising in general is but a relatively small part of children's cultural environment. There is also an issue of time lag in advertising bans. The call to ban advertising generally comes when something has become well-established over a long period of time. It took several generations for fast food to become so popular in the UK that it formed part of a national obesity epidemic. Advertising bans may have an effect, but probably not today, or even this decade. The effect of the advertising ban on cigarettes, for example, was hard to quantify. It prompted the industry to diversify its promotional efforts into sports sponsorship, sales promotion, and more innovative OOH billboard campaigns. Cigarette smoking has reduced considerably in the UK, but remains stubbornly popular amongst certain demographics, and is higher in the UK than some other Northern European countries. Banning HFSS advertising in children's TV programming has produced no discernable epidemiological effects to date, even though it has been shown that children may be seeing fewer fast food ads as a result. Advertising is but one of many marketing props in the cultural mise-en-scéne. Reducing the cultural presence of a consumption concept may well be a route to reducing consumption, but, as we have seen, much advertising takes a role in reassuring or reminding consumers, or it is simply aimed at retaining market share against competitors. It would take more than an advertising ban to reduce the cultural presence of high fat food in a UK food culture in which skills of cooking have declined along with the consciousness of what constitutes good food. What is needed is a radical change in British food culture.

## MAKING USE OF THE MAD MEN

The uses of marketing for promoting socially beneficial ends, as defined by the State, have still other difficulties associated with them. Turning the MadMen, those sinister Hidden Persuaders, away from the Dark Side to promote socially beneficial behavior, might seem an act of ecumenical wisdom. Governments need to promote business, and they need to promote health, wellbeing, and good citizenship. Bringing marketers in-house to address the social ills for which they are often blamed seems the magnanimous, and the smart thing to do. Redemption for all. But, there is a performative dimension to this. State-funded social marketing campaigns are effective PR for governments, because they present government as being in charge, aware of issues, and taking action. The government is not oversold in such campaigns, but everyone knows the source and the espoused motive for such campaigns. Government-backed social marketing campaigns are, in effect, content marketing for the state. What is more, governments that commission social marketing campaigns become clients of marketing, with the risks entailed of conflicts of interest. Which agencies get this business is a question that is sometimes answered by ministers who hold non-executive directorships or other links with the agencies that pitch for the brief. This doesn't necessarily mean that social marketing campaigns commissioned by government amount to mere propaganda. It does mean that the use of these campaigns is sensitive because there is a political element to State-sponsored social marketing, and a risk of self-interest confusing the aims. What if, say, £6 million earmarked for an anti-drinking TV campaign was used instead for treatment programmes for alcoholics? It could be that the number of problem drinkers helped would be greater, but there's little political capital to be earned from such a low profile, grass roots initiative.

There is yet another problem when governments commission high profile TV campaigns. Ad agencies that devise campaigns for commercial clients usually have a strategy, the success of which can be measured in terms of the campaign objectives. In social marketing, not only are outcomes more difficult to measure, but the cross-departmental wrangling involved in conceiving, planning, and executing social marketing campaigns can mean that the evaluation of the campaign becomes an afterthought, or gets forgotten altogether. The ad agency working on a commercial account is usually answerable to one person – the client, or the client's representative. This client has a piece of paper which has written on it the objectives that have been agreed for the campaign. These must dovetail into the client's marketing strategy. Government social marketing campaigns do not tend to have the management structure and accountability of commercial campaigns, and neither do they have the same clarity of objectives. Hence the aim can shift and the objectives can be fudged.

## YOUNG PEOPLE AND "SENSIBLE" DRINKING IN THE UK

The measurement of the success of government social marketing campaigns is a particularly fraught issue when it comes to anti-drinking campaigns. In 2004, I was one member of a four-person research team[10] investigating the role of alcohol in the lives of young adults. The UK government, in partnership with the world's biggest distiller *Diageo*, had commissioned a TV advertising campaign for Christmas 2006 to promote "sensible" drinking, and to dissuade young people from getting roaring drunk. Around this time, "binge" drinking (meaning getting very drunk for the fun of it) had become a front-page story in some newspapers, because of the scandalous behavior that was being seen in city and town centers every weekend. UK alcohol licensing laws had seen steady liberalization, with heavy investment in alcohol branding and advertising from the manufacturers. More retailers were allowed to sell alcohol, and more licensed venues were staying open for longer, culminating in the licensing Act of 2003, which came into force in 2005. Far from becoming a nation of "sensible" drinkers, sipping white wine and discussing the affairs of the day late into the evening over a leisurely plate of calamari, many British did what the British have always done: drink until we fall over, because we can. This, rather foreseeable, consequence of 24/7 alcohol sales created a panic in the media. Sensational stories linking youth drinking, crime, and social disorder became a staple of some populist newspapers. There was mounting pressure on the government to be seen to be doing something about this, but rolling back the licensing laws would be inconvenient for the alcohol manufacturers, who have a strong lobbying presence around government. An anti-drinking advertising campaign seemed to fit the bill.

When I saw the ads, I realized that this particular campaign was based on a mis-reading of youth drinking. The adverts showed young people being very drunk, with their peers showing disapproval and disowning them.[11] Older people watching the ad might read it as a message aimed at younger people that amounted to "if you get really drunk you might embarrass yourself and your friends." There was one small problem with this. My colleagues and I knew from our interviews with young people that the embarrassment of being very drunk was seen as part and parcel of the fun. Peers did not disapprove – in fact, the truth was quite the opposite. We had found in our research that many young adults drank to get very drunk indeed because this constituted them as "fun" people who did not put up a front but were prepared to let their guard down and reveal themselves to their friends at their most unflattering moments. This created "legendary" stories to talk about within the group.[12] These stories may have been humiliating on the face of it, embarrassing too, and even risky or shocking in some cases, but they were what great nights out were all about, and they bound the group closer in a drunken camaraderie. Getting very drunk was not an act of irresponsible nihilism – young drinkers were well aware of the risks of getting drunk in town centers. Doing so, though, made one vulnerable and heightened the mutual dependency of the group. Friends look out for each other, and heightening the risk intensifies the bond of friendship.

Given all that we had been told first hand by young people (who included non-drinkers too) in our research interviews, we realized that the ads actually represented a fun night out, not a bad one,[13] because of how embarrassingly funny the events of the night would seem when the story was re-told. We pointed out that the campaign wouldn't work, and national media in the UK picked up our research. I found myself interviewed on the radio with a senior *Diageo* official who argued that they were right because their research was better than ours.[14] I thought they'd completely missed the point with their sampling and data gathering approach. While the newspapers enjoyed our criticism of these advertisements, we were ignored at policy level and several subsequent campaigns were based on a similar, and similarly flawed creative strategy, namely, that if young people could see how they looked when drunk, they'd be embarrassed.

Of course, social marketing presents enough contradictions and potential conflicts of interest when used by governments, and these are multiplied when private sector partners are involved. Alcohol companies need to sell booze as effectively as possible, but they also have to negotiate the political need for CSR (Corporate Social Responsibility). Granted, the alcohol companies can't win, because however sincere their motives may be, they will be accused of tokenism, or of using social marketing to tick the CSR box. Regardless, it is clear that the contradictions of state-sponsored social marketing are by no means resolved when private sector partners are brought on board.

Five years after that campaign, and several subsequent ones, the topic of drinking is still at the top of the public health agenda in the UK, and there is a higher rate of liver cirrhosis amongst the under-thirties[15] than ever before. The point we made then, and repeatedly since, is that it isn't good enough for policy initiatives to use the tools of marketing to roll back the tide of social ills, unless the content of the marketing resonates with the consumer cultural context. Advertising has to have a kind of truth, in the sense that it has to connect emotionally with the target viewer. This is true of brand marketing, or "social" marketing. There must be something in the content of the communication that connects with the lived experience of the viewer. Ad agencies use a document they call the creative brief to translate the market insights they have into a creative execution that will activate the consumer.[16] The creative brief includes questions such as "what do we want the consumer to believe as a result of watching the ad?" and "why should they believe this?" If the ad portrays something that does not create a frisson of acknowledgement in the targeted viewer, it won't work. It wasn't true that young drinkers feel embarrassed at being very drunk, therefore the ads did not portray a truth.

There is little inherent power in marketing tools in themselves, despite what you might read in the countless social media marketing books pouring from the presses at the moment. Marketing effectiveness is about the content, in context. It's perfectly possible for companies to waste many millions on well-funded but ill-conceived marketing campaigns, and many do, every day. To put the anti-drinking social marketing campaigns in context, the reported £6 million spent on the 2007 anti-drinking campaign was in competition with an estimated £600–800 million annual marketing spend on alcohol in the UK,[17] or $2 billion in the USA. If you consider the cumulative marketing spend on alcohol across seven decades in the post-war era of mass broadcasting, a single social marketing campaign for safer drinking looks, well, like a drop in the barrel. Social marketing cannot compete with commercial marketing on scale, so it is even more important for it to reflect a genuine consumer cultural insight. For that, there has to be an understanding of the consumer cultural context. It simply wasn't true that young drinkers in the UK would meet with peer disapproval from their friendship group if they got hopelessly drunk. We'd spoken with groups of 18–25 year olds, who had told us their stories. It turned out that *Diageo* had done a much bigger research study than ours, but it had been a survey rather than personal interviews; it had included respondents in Europe as well as the UK, and the sample had included people aged up to 35.[18] At 35, one's espoused lifestyle and values are pretty different to the ones you share informally with your friends at 21. Leaving aside the political expediency for the government and the alcohol industry in blaming alcohol problems on young, irresponsible individuals, the campaign simply didn't connect with the lived experience of young people who used alcohol in their social lives.

## MY ENCOUNTER WITH A POLICY NUDGER

Government social marketing on alcohol and health may be clumsily well-meaning, but, like many social marketing campaigns, it lacks the sharpness of insight and clarity of purpose that drive commercial brand marketing campaigns. One young policy wonk I met at a Whitehall Department of Health meeting on alcohol policy in 2012 realized this. He used to work in commercial branding before he became a policy advisor working for the Behavioral Insights Team – also known as the "nudge" unit – attached to the Prime Minister's Cabinet Office. At his request I helped him to put together a briefing paper for civil servants that engaged with the brand positioning strategies of alcohol companies. He knew well enough that the same alcohol brands tend to feature in studies of what young "binge" drinkers like to use to get drunk. These brands, like all the others, ostensibly adhere to the many rules on alcohol marketing. But brand commu- nication is not just about explicit messages – it is also about understanding the implicit dimension of brands, the tacit behaviors, values, and associations that the brand signifies to its target group. Few people are aware of this socio-cultural level of brand meaning, other than the people who manage the brand, and the target audience.

My policy advising colleague understood very well that internal (and inevitably confidential) brand positioning documents focus on the connotations of brands, the implicit meanings. Alcohol branding has become more sophisti- cated and assumed a far greater scale over the past 30 years. Alcohol branding is leveraged by alcohol's ambivalent social status as a marker of conviviality, and also a marker of trans- gression. For young people, drinking has an obvious trans- gressive appeal,[19] in keeping with the ambivalent cultural meaning of alcohol itself. In the past decade, a great deal of alcohol branding has traded on transgressive undertones. In 2006 the UK regulator, the Advertising Standards Authority, tightened up its code of practice to be stricter on alcohol ads that seemed to appeal to young drinkers by associating drinking with sexual or social success, or with adolescent humor. Like the cigarette companies when cigarette advertising became more tightly regulated in the 1980s, though, the alcohol brands simply adopted subtler symbolism[20] and more nuanced strategies.

In many consumption practices, people like to feel that they're asserting their own individuality by symbolically transgressing or breaking a norm or taboo. Some brands know how to tacitly position themselves to exploit that deepest of consumer motivations. Of course, brands would be unlikely to concede that that is what they do. Drinking, and especially drinking to get drunk, simultaneously fulfils a dual need for sociability, and taboo-breaking. Alcohol has always opened the door to social bonding in many cultures by leveling social hierarchies and symbolising a "time out" of official life and the restrictions of social structure. At the same time, drinking has a transgressive frisson, but in a way that is also acceptable to peers. Every government proclamation to drink "sensibly" and "responsibly," and every newspaper splash about Britain's binge drinking problem, serve to reassert and magnify the sense that drinking is one way we can still place ourselves beyond the reach of stifling social rules and norms, and enjoy a brief experience of intoxicating carnival freedom. In a suffocating climate of surveillance, self-control and moral disapproval, it is one taboo we're still allowed to break. It is a powerful appeal and the brands know how to exploit it by carefully calculating the implicit connotations of the brand. They develop their brand strategy by considering not only the regulations on alcohol marketing but also the cultural mise-en-scéne of their consumers.

In Chapter 2, I alluded to the way the most commonly known theories of persuasive communication in marketing ignore the implicit dimension. A 1950s print ad for a car might show a happy, attractive family enjoying a day out in a new *Buick*, with a strapline proclaiming the reliability of the car. The implicit message, though, associates the lifestyle, and the happy family, with ownership of the car. In marketing, as in rhetoric, the persuasive force of what is not explicitly stated can be considerable. It is axiomatic that 90% of human communication is non-verbal. Similarly, in marketing, much of the meaning drawn from communications is implicit, rather than explicit. Some brands know how to exploit this, even if they cannot control it. *Nike*, for example, was positioned as a specialist sports brand for aspiring and elite athletes, until Los Angeles gangs began to wear the brand as street wear in the 1980s. The association with transgression, rule-breaking, and street toughness was soon absorbed into the brand positioning. I am not suggesting that brands knowingly promote law-breaking or anti-social behavior. They're just doing what comes naturally to brand planners. Their business is to understand the cultural meanings that consumers read into the brand, and they use that knowledge to connect with their target consumers. Branding is a semiotic chess game played with symbolic pieces.

To digress, the more you think about this implicit aspect of branding, the more unlikely it starts to seem. Take German car brands – today, they're amongst the most powerful symbols of Western freedom one can find, but they had to outgrow some rather unpromising historical baggage. Given that individualism, even in the West, retains an intrinsically transgressive note since it implies divergence from the social group, this works well on an implicit level for brands. I have to admit that I probably feel younger, more attractive, and more exciting than I really am when I'm driving my second-hand BMW 630i. After all, James Bond drives them. I don't think about the historical role of German car brands in the Second World War.[21] My point here is to underline the socially constructed character of brands. They subsist not only in the factories in which they're put together and in the tangibility of the product and logo, but partly in the social spaces between people. This socially constructed element of brands becomes detached from history. Hence, in a sense, brands are cultural figments, although their meaning and symbolism are real enough for consumers.

It would be unreasonable to suggest that brands with transgressive notes in their positioning are encouraging social harm or disorder. In any case, they cannot impose their chosen meaning on culture without the tacit complicity of consumers. However, regulators and policy makers ought to acknowledge the scope of marketing signification in brand positioning strategies. Brand positioning documents are typically very candid about the underlying meaning their marketing strategies exploit. My government collaborator had the bright idea that if brands had to concede the true nature of their positioning, they could be persuaded by moral force to manage it more responsibly. In other words, if they knew that the regulators and legislators actually understood how marketing worked on an implicit level, they would have to take their social responsibility seriously. But before the regulators could be persuaded to engage with the cultural semiotics of alcohol brands, the paper had to get the relevant civil servants on board. I haven't heard from him, so I guess the idea didn't take off.

It was always going to be a hard sell. The cultural dimension of marketing cannot easily be articulated, at least not in the mechanistic terms in which people are accustomed to thinking about marketing. Brand positioning can be represented on a graphic to make it seem concrete, and it can be itemized in lists of connotations that spring from each brand. Some brand consultants call this a "metaphorical analysis." Brands are anthropomorphized and their human-like qualities accentuated in branding and communication, in order to try to cue emotional responses from consumers. In the end, a brand is an abstract and contingent notion that cannot easily be conceived separately from its consumer cultural context. The meaning of a brand is always contingent on what people are saying and thinking about it, and brand marketers use emic, insider-perspective research techniques to understand the meanings brands have in their consumer cultural context.

Brand marketers know how to conceive of an ad that meets the regulations on one level, yet also resonates with the target consumer's wish to symbolically transform their identity. The regulators are fixated on a legalistic interpretation of explicit marketing communications. They dare not stray into the semiotic quicksands of cultural interpretation. The task of my colleague and I was to tell a bunch of civil servants that some alcohol marketing tacitly colludes in excessive drinking by building the transgressive pleasures of alcohol into the brand positioning. It might have been like trying to tell an American senator in the 1960s that smoking could be reduced if more people understood how the Marlboro Man image tacitly linked smoking with a myth of rugged American masculinity. Administrators and politicians don't generally think like that.

Context shapes every question in marketing, and every answer. The cultural context of youth drinking, and specifically the social role of alcohol in young peoples' lives, was not understood by the government, and this resulted in a naive creative proposition dooming an expensive advertising campaign to failure. This judgment may sound a bit smug – the brief was unquestionably difficult and the campaign was, no doubt, well intended. What is more, our research showed that these ads wouldn't work – it didn't tell us which kinds of ads *would* work. We maintained that alcohol policy needed to be founded on stronger, and truer, insights about the cultural meaning of drinking and drunkenness, but that's no prescription for success in itself. In any case, it would be naive to think that one campaign could reverse 400 years of British alcohol culture. The idea that greater availability and longer serving hours would result in an outbreak of "sensible" continental drinking was never very likely, given Britain's centuries of battles with the bottle. Alcohol today has a greater cultural presence in the UK than ever before. Through sports and music event sponsorship, online content including games and counter-culturally themed advertising, alcohol brands are vividly represented in UK culture. The prominence of alcohol brands in retail promotions, with the promotions activated by pyramids of booze piled high throughout the stores, is testimony of the power of alcohol brands to get customers through supermarket doors. The high level of cultural presence, along with 24/7 availability and the lowest real-terms cost ever known, means that it is more difficult than ever before for anyone with an alcohol problem in the UK to avoid temptation.

## IMPLICIT MEANING AND ADVERTISING REGULATION

Perhaps it isn't realistic for advertising regulation to engage with the finer points of brand semiotics. The problem is, the mis-match in understanding means the regulators and the marketers are entwined in a game of cat and mouse that is satisfactory for neither. The regulators apply literal, legalistic interpretation to marketing communications, focusing only on what is explicitly stated in the ad. This binds advertising more tightly in regulatory bureaucracy. As more and more regulations are applied, the brands find this onerous and stifling of innovation. Nonetheless, it has the effect of forcing them to develop more subtle techniques.

In one example to illustrate the difficulty of regulating for implicit meaning, I was asked by a food pressure group to comment on an advertisement used by a UK bread manufacturer, *Allinson*. The ad juxtaposed a picture of hands kneading dough with the phrase, "*Allinson* Today," even though the bread is made with modern production methods and not by the Victorian methods implied in the ad. The *Real Bread Campaign*, a food lobby group, protested to the regulator, the Advertising Standards Authority that the ad was potentially misleading, and I agreed, but their complaint was dismissed. The ad did not explicitly claim that it was made by a Victorian whole food technique, so the ASA was unwilling to rule that the ad contravened its code of practice.[22] In my view, and that of the RBC, there was a clearly implied suggestion in the ad. The whole look of the ad, with sepia coloring and images that evinced the Victorian origins of the brand, suggested that the brand positioning strategy was to tap into a Romantic idea of the better food quality of years ago, and to play down the chemical content and mass production methods of modern bread manufacturing. The truth was that the bread was not made in the Victorian way, but by modern scientific methods. Then again, it has to be conceded that branding and advertising play with cultural meaning in ways that are extremely difficult for regulators to second guess. Consumers complete the meaning of a brand Gestalt, not regulators. Had the regulators agreed that the ad made an implicit suggestion that was misleading, it could have opened up a Pandora's Box of conflicts over the implicit meaning of advertisements.

## MARKETING AND SYMBOLISM

There is a widespread habit of thinking about marketing not as a cultural intervention, but as a boxes-and-arrows mechanism that targets consumers with rational appeals based on product utility. This was true only of a proportion of marketing back in 1959 when Sidney J. Levy published "Symbols for Sale" in the *Harvard Business Review*.[23] The marketing academy chose to relegate Levy's anthropological insight to the margins of marketing studies, while much of the anthropological and sociological work in marketing gravitated to the parallel discipline of consumer research.[24] In effect, marketing abdicated its position as the business discipline that articulates the voice of the consumer in the organization. In the idiom I've chosen for this book, I argue that the cultural force of marketing practice, and the lived experience of consumers, can be better understood by thinking of marketing as an activity that invariably operates within a dynamic and shifting context. The marketing professional has to try to commission or design content that, artfully placed, will shape the consumer's mise-en-scéne. What this does is to move conceptualizations of marketing practice away from the cue-ball cause-effect mentality fostered by much business school marketing teaching, and toward a broader appreciation of the cultural context of marketing.

The symbolism of marketing may be difficult for regulators to accommodate, but the examples above hint at the depth of knowledge of consumer culture that is needed to articulate brands in ways that resonate with consumers. Intervening in the socio-cultural mise-en-scéne in ways that will engage and activate consumers demands a nuanced, emic understanding of what brands mean in local consumer cultural contexts. This is difficult enough for commercial marketers, but more difficult still for state institutions with the aim not of maintaining market share, but of changing behavior. Despite the difficulties, if marketing is to be more widely understood, the implicit and symbolic aspects of marketing have to become a standard part of the way the topic is discussed, thought about, theorized, and taught. The top brands understand marketing signification because they understand the cultural context in which they operate. Regulators, students, managers, and researchers should aspire to a similar level of understanding. Their task is to understand the world consumers occupy as a three-dimensional mise-en-scéne.

# CHAPTER 6

# Consumer Agency and Brand Culture

## MARKET STRUCTURE AND BRANDS

Are we consumers sad little sheep being herded about by the not-so-good marketing shepherds? Or are we in control of our own thoughts and behavior? In this chapter I want to explore some perspectives on this question of human social study. To put it more generally: are we made by social structure, or do we make ourselves? This question, never addressed in typical marketing courses, is central to marketing practice. If marketing professionals are to try to influence and control consumer behavior, do they try to engage with our reason as autonomous, thinking individuals? Or, should they try to frame our choices by manipulating the social structures, the broader cultural contexts, that frame what we are and how we behave, in the belief that where others go the rest will follow? I may have given the impression in parts of this book that I have pre-empted the answer. I advocate an appreciation of marketing effects at a consumer cultural level. However, I don't feel that this necessarily precludes individual sovereignty. In other words, the answer to the question I posed above is, "it depends." At the heart of the human problem of structure versus agency, is a contradiction. We think of ourselves as individuals, but our individuality is defined relationally. Similarly, as consumers, we think of our choice of brands as an expression of our individual identity, yet brand symbolism means nothing in a social vacuum. In other words, we need other people to partake in and validate the identity games we play with brands. There is, then, a dialectical relationship between structure and agency, and part of the job of marketers is to understand the dynamics of this dialectic with regard to particular consumer markets.

One kind of structural power with which a contextualized approach to marketing has to contend is market power. Many markets today are oligopolistic, with a dozen or so major companies dominating the major part of market share. What does this mean for marketing management? Consumer choice is never infinite, and we understand that. We cannot dictate terms to suppliers, even though many companies now try to offer bespoke services, to a degree. But to what extent are our choices delimited by the market power of suppliers? Lateral mergers and a policy of producing multiple brands for the same categories of product have concentrated many consumer markets to the extent that a small number of global multinationals control a large number of the most familiar brands. Clearly, influence over consumer mises-en-scéne is more easily attained when the manufacturer has deep pockets for funding product development, marketing, research, sponsorship and content development, not to mention for lobbying governments on competition or consumer legislation, or indeed for buying out competition. Does market dominance make the marketing job easy?

Certainly, consumer goods suppliers seem keen to increase industrial concentration by buying out competitors. On a global scale, corporations including *Coca Cola*, *PepsiCo*, *P&G*, *Nestlé*, *Mondelez International*, *Kellogg's*, *Mars*, *Johnson & Johnson*, *General Mills*, *Colgate Palmolive* and *Unilever* account for a high proportion of the most well-known household cleaning, food, confectionary, beverages, and personal care brands.[1] For example, *Colgate Palmolive* have scores of oral hygiene, personal care, and food brands including *Ajax*, *Palmolive*, and *Ultrabrite*. *Mondelez International* includes the countless confectionary and convenience food brands of *Kraft* and *Cadbury*. *Nestlé* is familiar for its coffee and chocolate confections but also has a stake in *L'Oréal* and its range of high fashion clothing and cosmetics including *Hugo Boss*, *Ralph Lauren*, *Georgio Armani*, and *Diesel*. *P&G*'s portfolio of hundreds of household consumer brands includes *Gillette*, *Pantene*, *Duracell*, *Braun*, *Tide*, and *Oral-B*. *Unilever* chips in with *Dove*, *Axe*, *Ben & Jerry's*, *Pot Noodle*, *Magnum*, *Vaseline*, and *Ponds*, amongst scores of other iconic household brands. The famously ascetic *Mr Kellogg's* modern day conglomerate gives us the world's best-selling breakfast cereal *Special K*, along with *Corn Flakes* (of course), *Green Giant* corn, and *Nutri Grain*, while *Mars* gives us pet foods, chocolate confections, and chewing gum brands galore.

Corporate structures are legal entities in which brands operate as independent businesses, operating under the corporate umbrella. Some use "family" brand names to identify the corporation with the brand, as with many *Nestlé* products, but others, such as *Unilever*, rarely do. Brands are bigger than corporations in the sense that it is the brands that consumers connect with and pay for, not the corporation. Many brands began as small independents before succumbing to the need for scale and being bought up by bigger businesses. Their new owners need them to continue to maintain the identity that consumers recognize and value. There has been much talk of brand equity in recent years as an accounting concept that values the intangible brand, as distinct from the physical assets, on balance sheets. The logic of brand equity is that brands are free-standing and enduring sources of revenue, regardless of who happens to be the legal owner of the manufacturing plant or the trademark. The capital, plant, and machinery may be necessary to the manufacture of the brand, but it doesn't matter to the consumer how, where, or by whom the brand is made. It is the brand itself as a social construction that subsists, in effect, as a quasi monopolistic business, in the sense that consumers will seek it out and pay a higher price for it than we would for an unbranded alternative. A brand is seen as an asset as concrete, in terms of revenue, as the factory, and many have a good deal more longevity.

## BRAND EXTENSIONS

The same logic drives brand extensions. A successful brand is a barrier to market entry for potential rivals because it sets the marketing expenditure bar very high for new entrants. It can also be a means of entry into new markets for the brand owner, because of the symbolic cultural currency it carries. The guaranteed recognition can ease the way into a new market, when a new and unknown brand would have to struggle, and spend a lot of money, to be accepted. The newly entered market does not necessarily have to be related to the original brand's market, for example where *Marlboro* cigarettes and *Harley Davidson* motorcycles have introduced licensed clothing lines and sports holdalls. These are pretty familiar by now, but there are plenty of extensions that have looked incongruous, on the face of it at least, such as *Marlboro* beer, *Kellogg's* clothes, *Louis Vuitton* watches, and *Everlast* energy bars, not to mention *Virgin* funerals and *Donald Trump – The Fragrance*. When we are children we get excited when we recognize things, and this pleasure at recognition never quite leaves us. In an age of global travel and communication, brands have become a shared symbolic vocabulary. Consumers like what we like, and we go back to the same, well-recognized brands again and again. It feels reassuring, somehow. I recall a market test long ago when a famous brand was re-packaged in a different color. No one liked it. Today, consumers have become more fluent in brand signification and seem happier to engage in play with the brand symbolism. This gives brands a license to extend, and a means of entering new markets. For example, for many decades, *Ribena* was marketed in the UK as a blackcurrant cordial, to be mixed with water. The brand was inconceivable in any other form or flavor. It eventually moved into pre-mixed drinks, and relatively recently launched strawberry and mango and lime flavors.

Naturally, there is a need for owners to manage the provision of the brand so that it continues to make sense to consumers. The 80-year-old *Kit Ka*t,[2] for example, has been the best selling "countline" (a chocolate covered confection usually with added ingredient such as biscuit) in the UK for more than 50 years. In the past decade there have been many extensions of the original iconic red package, milk chocolate version into different flavors and formats and different colors of pack. Some of these have been a success, others not. When Swiss conglomerate *Nestlé* controversially[3] took over British *Kit Kat* manufacturer *Rowntree Mackintosh* in 1988, they wanted *Rowntree* brands, rather than the Yorkshire factory, so a large proportion of the circa £2 billion price tag was for "goodwill," for the intangible asset of the brands. *Rowntree* had a roster of well-established and top-selling brands including *Fruit Gums*, *Smarties*, and *Polo Mints* as well as *Kit Kat*. These had the potential to grow more significantly in international markets. This was exactly what *Nestlé* were looking for. Industrial concentration has made it expensive and difficult for new brands to succeed in established consumer markets. As I note above, the prohibitive marketing costs for new start-ups act as a barrier to entry for any manufacturer without marketing resources. Developing the existing history and recognition of an established brand, in order to expand its presence internationally, carries a lower risk and higher return than starting from scratch with a brand new product. *Kit Kat* sales growth has continued on a global scale under *Nestlé*'s ownership, notwithstanding a few hiccups along the way.

## DOES CONCENTRATED BRAND OWNERSHIP LIMIT CONSUMER FREEDOM?

The dense concentration of ownership in many consumer brand markets looks startling on the face of it. It raises the question of the extent to which consumers can live their everyday lives without becoming a revenue stream for big business. In other words, can consumers escape the market?[4] Many would say not. Some would say that these few conglomerates "control" our choices to an alarming degree. I would hesitate to advance industrial concentration in consumer markets as support for an argument that consumers lack real choice or are "controlled" by a faceless industrial complex. I feel that would be going too far, but equally it is quite mistaken to overplay the autonomy and sovereignty of the consumer, given that many markets are oligopolistic, with a dozen or so major suppliers dominating the scene. To say that consumer choices, tastes, and preferences are framed and cued by marketing simply reflects the social influence on all behavior. Culture primes our beliefs and behavior within the realm of consumption, or outside it. Human autonomy occurs in the interstices of social structure, and I feel that consumption as a field can facilitate our senses of autonomy and agency, or inhibit them. As ever, it is a matter of looking at cases in their context. I'm no apologist for corporatism but I think it is simplistic to argue that the market structure for consumer goods is intrinsically wrong or anti-sovereignty. The market structure has, after all, arisen partly out of our own choices.

Humans use objects for symbolic social purposes, and brands act as a powerful symbolic currency. Consumers do not have to be passive automatons or dupes.[5] Marketing signs are not hegemonic – we can resist, ignore, or re-interpret them. We use, adapt, co-opt, activate, and integrate brands in our social lives, often with creativity and verve. Some of us join in consumer cultural groups such as surfers, sports fans, Harry Potter-ettes, bikers, boy racers, outdoorsmen, Star Trekkies, mods, new agers, streetcar modifiers, street dancers, or any of countless other consumer quasi-communities, to express our sense of freedom from the sanitized lifestyles sold to us by the corporate machine. This engagement can be physical, virtual, or both. Many of us engage actively with brands, rather than passively acquiescing to their hegemony over our lives. Brands are part of the ebb and flow of cultural currents.

Consumers can, in any case, exercise some creativity even where they lack relative power. Computer and video games, for example, are often regarded as things that have had an unequivocally negative influence on children's development. They distract children from their schoolwork, induce them to stay up too late, give them an excuse not to play outside and get exercise, and they discourage them from social interaction, or so the argument goes. Yet it is not so simple. No doubt all those negative effects can come to pass, in the right circumstances or through a lack of adequate family guidance. However, children have integrated their use of video games and digital technology into the changing currents of their lives to reflect and articulate their increased autonomy as consumers, their increased power in family decision making, and the changing patterns and demands of their leisure activities and social lives.[6] They have used computer games to improve their cognitive and motor skills, and they have deployed digital technology as a means of facilitating and extending their social lives. Computer games are toys to children, and children have always played with toys in innovative ways. Children are not necessarily passive consumers, but active and creative ones. As a parent myself, I am not suggesting that video and computer games are unconditionally positive parts of children's lives, nor am I suggesting that they can replace other developmental activities. My point is simply that even children can, and do, exercise active creativity within their own group consumption practices.

## THE INDIVIDUAL AND THE GROUP

Some contemporary marketing campaigns try to engage consumers on several levels in order to create the sense that the marketing offer is an invitation to the consumer to exercise their own creativity, within a community. For example, German sportswear brand *Puma* launched a UK campaign in March 2013 called "Worn My Way," aimed at capturing consumers' own senses of creativity. The campaign signed up urban music stars and includes a microsite, social media activity, a dedicated YouTube channel for related content including "behind-the-scenes" film featuring the stars, a competition for consumers to respond to the question "what does it mean to be yourself?"[7] and experiential sports and music events scheduled for the summer.[8] The concept evokes the creative individual of Western Romanticism, but the individual is constituted, without apparent contradiction, in terms of the group. The group, of course, is constituted in terms of the brand. The sense of creative individuality that is the basis of the appeal, is not autonomous, but relational. The "behind-the-scenes" video shows an advertisement apparently being made, with young, hip models wearing *Puma* clothing and shoes as they are photographed in urban street scenes. They are not *Vogue* models but have a somewhat Bohemian look, reflecting the motif of creative individualism against an implicitly rejected high fashion industry. But, these are not nonconformists whose creativity sets them outside social structure. They are leaders in style who find their creative expression through the symbols conferred on them by *Puma*.

The campaign theme echoes a recent trend for major brands to appoint celebrity performers like Lady Gaga, Justin Timberlake, and Taylor Swift as "creative director" or "brand manager."[9] The assumption is that the celebrity brings their own creative leadership to add a greater authenticity to the brand than would be the case with a clichéd and patently insincere celebrity "endorsement." So, the dialectical interplay of structure and agency is woven through the *Puma* campaign concept. But, just because a campaign evokes myths of creative individualism through signs and symbols,[10] it does not mean that consumers will necessarily respond. The campaign invites the engagement of a self-defined target group from amongst the young, urban and style-conscious. Whatever they do to respond, if they do at all, their behavior as consumers will be self-defined, according to the terms of the campaign. Consumer culture binds us into a lifestyle defined by marketers, unless they grant us the tools to craft our own postmodern liberation.[11]

## ETHICAL ISSUES OF MARKET POWER

The interplay of social structure and consumer agency becomes particularly fraught in areas of social policy where there is tension between whole population measures, and targeted measures. If I eat unhealthily, smoke cigarettes or drink too much beer, who is to blame? Me? Or is it all the fault of those nasty marketing folk? For example, in UK alcohol policy, also discussed in Chapter 5, this issue is often presented starkly in terms of the rights of the majority of "responsible" drinkers not to have to suffer penalties because of the "irresponsibility," or alcoholism, of the few, when whole population measures such as tax rises are proposed. The polarization of the debate has succeeded in paralyzing UK alcohol policy for several decades, while liberalization of alcohol licensing and booming investment in alcohol brands has changed the business radically, shifting large chunks of consumption from pubs and licensed premises, into retail "off" sales. Since the policy decision was made to treat alcohol like any other grocery item,[12] rising rates of alcohol-related disease and connected social problems like street crime and disorder have caused protest from medical lobbies, assisted by sensationalized coverage of city-centre drinking from certain newspapers. The refrain from the industry, though, supported by government, has been that it is the individual who controls their consumption. Of course, this is true, but it is also predictable that a hugely increased scale of alcohol branding will stimulate a longer tail of alcohol-related social and health ills. Alcohol is marketed as an essential accessory to a fun social life.[13] As we saw in Chapter 5, drinking excessively within the group both subverts the marketing machine, and serves it. For theorists like Theodore Adorno or Guy Debord, popular culture, in which we can include marketing, can be seen to dominate and subjugate human nature. In other words, the social structure obliterates agency. In contrast to this position, it could be argued that structure and agency can both be at work through consumption.

The market operates within a framework of legal and voluntary regulation, but there is still much room for interpretation of regulations, as we saw with the *Allinson* example in the previous chapter. For example, alcohol advertising on TV is not supposed to appeal to under-18s, according to the code of practice. This, though, is very much a matter of subjective judgment, and many pre-schoolers will, when asked, recite alcohol brands amongst their favorite TV ads. Forty years ago in the UK, alcohol ads on TV were set in pubs or other drinking spaces, and the actors looked very middle aged. Alcoholism and drunkenness were social issues as they are today, but drinking was not a major preoccupation of policy or media debate. Today, many brands of alcohol and, indeed, many other brands ostensibly targeted at adults, such as financial services and cars, are branded with quirky, offbeat ads and cartoon or puppet characters that are clearly very attractive to children, despite the ASA code of practice. De-regulation and the infantilization[14] of alcohol marketing have, arguably, widened the market for alcohol consumption[15] and inflamed the problems at the margins, but the alcohol manufacturers naturally prefer the deregulated market. Incidentally, branding for many goods and services targeted at adults, not just alcohol, are brighter, more whimsical, and more childlike in their imagery than they were in the 1970s, so it is hard to lay the blame for this solely with alcohol brands.

More recently, there has been as much concern over the marketing of processed food. In the UK, as in several other developed nations, especially the USA, an obesity epidemic has become a policy priority because of the link between obesity and many other negative health indicators. Concerns over childhood obesity rates prompted the ban on UK TV advertising for HFSS foods in children's TV programming in 2007,[16] and there are daily media stories about the cost to the UK NHS of rising rates of diabetes, gastric by-pass operations and other, related public costs including the cost of treating obesity-related cancers, heart disease and disability, and associated welfare costs.

The debates about the primary causes of obesity tend to focus on the ubiquity of fast food chain restaurants in British towns and cities, the high sugar and/or fat content of heavily marketed processed foods and fizzy drinks sold in super-markets, lack of exercise, and a cultural loss of cooking skills and dietary knowledge. Food manufacturers and retailers are often in the front line of criticism for misleading promotion and food labeling that presents food as more healthy than it really is. They might argue that one *MacDonald*'s or *Burger King* a week or one can of *Coke* hurts no one, but why, they might say, should they be held responsible for the minority who drink ten cans a day or eat ten burgers a week? On the other hand, health lobbyists would maintain that the fast food producers use a whole population approach to sell their product by advertising on a mass scale, so why would govern-ments use a targeted approach to deal with the unintended consequences? For health lobbyists, whole population measures such as advertising bans or fat taxes make sense, even though there might be a cost in jobs.

Market power can lead to other problems besides over-consumption. Where suppliers dominate the market they tend to force down price throughout the supply chain. This benefits consumers through lower prices, but it also creates pressure on suppliers to cut corners. In March 2013, there were scandals in the UK and Europe about the processed food supply chain when it was discovered that major national supermarkets had been retailing products labeled as beef that actually contained horse and pork (also noted in Chapter 1). Processed food buying has become far removed from its production, and branding and marketing have assumed great importance in framing food choices. Many consumers today have little awareness about the origins of their food – some eat chicken nuggets every day but have never seen a live chicken, and wouldn't know that a large proportion of chickens eaten in the UK are sourced from overseas. Neither would most people know that the chicken nugget supply chain is as globalised as the one for processed beef products, meaning no one is quite sure what's in them.[17] The definition of "chicken" or "beef" used by food regulators can be pretty quirky, including skin, sinew, even feathers. Many other consumers are unaware of the huge amounts of sugar, fat, and chemical additives added to typical processed meals, fizzy drinks, and foodstuffs.

Supermarkets are cathedrals of plenty, and everything sold is packaged and branded to maintain the myth of happy abundance. The presentation and branding of foods insulates the consumer from the grimy reality of the labor and manufacturing process and the distant supply chain. Of course, there is consumer passivity as well as activism. In the UK we have crowded like zombies into prefabricated super-markets to buy processed ready meals, and the footfall in our historical high streets has slowed to a trickle. We can take our car and stuff everything we need for the week into one big shopping expedition, leaving more time for watching TV. For "we" read "me" – I have to admit, I love supermarkets. The abundance is just intoxicating.

## THE UK'S FAST FOOD CULTURE

There are other aspects to the unfortunate confluence of cultural influences in Britain's problem with food and fat. Many households no longer eat meals together at the table, but instead snack and graze on convenience processed foods perched on the couch while watching TV. Many other house-holds no longer cook, but microwave-ready meals bought pre-prepared from the supermarket, or they buy take-away fast food. The historical context is that the UK, arguably, does not have as strong a culture of fresh food preparation and cooking as many other European countries. Neither do we have as strong a culture of social cooking and eating, with the family, as in Mediterranean Europe. Many of us watch cooking shows on TV from our living room couch instead, while spooning a microwave-ready meal out of its polystyrene container.

During the post-war period in the UK, home frying of food in poorer households became the norm, while the lack of salt, butter, and lard during the war and for some time afterwards resulted in many baby boomers acquiring a habit of over-indulgence when these condiments and dairy products became plentiful again. Habits such as adding spoons of sugar and full fat milk to hot black tea, putting salt in boiling vegetables, and then adding more salt as a seasoning to meals, became deeply ingrained. At meal times in my youth my father would angrily condemn my brother and I for cutting the fat off our slices of the Sunday beef joint. When he was growing up during war rationing, people needed all the calories they could get, and animal fat was prized as an energy source. He felt that cutting fat off meat was a waste of good food. Our national taste for salt and fat seems to have continued. Into this stew of bad habits we can throw the urbanisation of populations and the concomitant rise of supermarkets to dominate food supply, while many local butchers, fishmongers, bread makers and milk suppliers have disappeared. Moreover, demographic changes have influenced food consumption. There is now a greater number of single person households than ever before in the UK, and more women go out to work. The ritual of the nuclear family sitting down to dinner is unknown in many dwellings. Convenience and microwaved meals have become big sellers, and downward pressure on food prices has driven the management of the processed food supply chain into sourcing the cheapest possible ingredients, wherever they happen to come from, culminating in the horse meat scandal.[18] Even more worrying, there have been reports in the UK press of some schools in low income areas having to provide breakfast as well as lunch for rising numbers of children because, it seems, their parents don't understand what real food is, and think a packet of biscuits or some cold potato chips serve as a meal.[19]

The manufacturers, then, of processed food and carbonated drinks operate within a context of historical and cultural facts. They supply high sugar, high fat, easily prepared food and drink, because that's what we like. To be sure, there is a good deal of venality in the labeling. Claims of "low fat" are seldom qualified with "but we've sweetened it with half a bag of sugar instead." Debates about food and drink labeling, though, operate within a wider context. They matter, but they cannot be seen as causal elements in themselves. The root cause of obesity is people being unable to cope with being hungry, then eating high calorie food that doesn't really satisfy them. A Chinese student in one of my classes once summed up British food. She said "it fills my stomach, but it does not fill my mind." We've brutalized our taste buds with chips, salt, sugar, and white bread, and we feed our hunger with high density calories that lack the bulk or the complexity of taste to satisfy us for long. Supermarkets stock fresh fish, vegetables, and other wholesome foods, but many of us choose the processed food instead, and not only for cost, but often because we don't have the skills or the patience to prepare meals from scratch.

Whole population measures such as enforced reductions in fat or sugar content of processed food, or smaller portion sizes in take-away carbonated drinks, might have an effect that would reflect in better epidemiological figures for obesity across the population in the long term, but they wouldn't address the low cultural priority large numbers of British people give to healthy eating. For people acculturated into carb-laden HFSS foods and without cooking skills, healthy foods seem boring. Food manufacturers and retailers have a moral and legal duty to provide food with edible and clearly labeled ingredients, and to make their supply chain processes transparent so that consumers can make an informed choice. They are, though, confined by the food culture into which they are selling. This isn't to excuse marketers who sell products that are damaging to health or of dubious provenance. They make their decisions, ethical or not, but when shareholder value is driving corporate rationality there are only two safeguards against poor food standards – government oversight and consumer education.

A third, good investigative journalism can be important too, in supporting the second.

## MARKETING'S STRUGGLE WITH CULTURE

Marketing, then, entails an engagement with cultures of consumption. It seldom enjoys the power to impose new cultural values that are alien to those that are already there. Even Edward Bernays's PR efforts, influential though they proved, had to dovetail into a receptive cultural context. His programme to make public smoking acceptable for women would probably have failed were it not for the democratizing effect the Second World War had on gender roles. This version of the "culture has strategy for breakfast" thesis applies across national cultures as well as within them. For example, *Tesco*, the supermarket chain, has expanded internationally but it has adapted its product lines, merchandising, and service to fit with prevailing buying habits in different countries. *Tesco Lotus*,[20] its operation in Thailand and South East Asia, has had to adapt its offer in that region because there is resistance to buying frozen and processed foods. The habit of buying and cooking fresh foods from markets remains strong, and the store had to employ adapted merchandising and stock approaches. In addition, there is an expectation of personal service in South East Asian retail settings, whereas in the West we're now used to weighing our own produce, filling our own shopping bags and even acting as our own check-out clerk. *Tesco*, the world's third biggest retailer,[21] were less successful in expanding into the USA, where their franchise *Fresh & Easy* has been written off as a failure.

Chain restaurants, too, have to adapt to local cultures. *McDonald*'s restaurants around the world have a different menu, depending on the country. True, one could say that the strategy has begun to change culture in some respects, because there are reports of rising obesity rates in South East Asian countries where Western fast food outlets and retailers have become established. These obesity rates, though, still lag far behind those of the West and must be understood within a wider context of rising affluence and greater exposure to Western culture in general. Rituals and practices of food consumption are deeply acculturated, and marketing is but one part of the food consumers' mises-en-scéne. It exerts an influence, but within a wider cultural context. Marketing does not stand apart from culture, looking in from the outside, performing manipulative operations like a scientist molding the behavior of laboratory rats. It is part of the same culture, and the most effective marketers understand how to embrace the complexity of that cultural context.

It is important to raise questions over the quality of marketing consumers get. Unethical marketing has an easy time where consumers are passive. Consumers have to make active and informed choices in order for markets to respond in ways that we want. Markets respond to the things consumers do, not to the things we say. From a marketing perspective, the mise-en-scéne is easier to arrange if there is less competition to distract the consumers' attention. But if food companies have understood the consumer cultural context so well that they are able to provide a ready-made lasagne meal for £1 that just needs two minutes in a microwave, then they can hardly be condemned for that. A lot of thinking, planning, sourcing, and science go into these products. Some of them turned out to contain a little-itty bit of horsemeat: they're still remarkable feats of food marketing, whatever they're made of. In the end, the consumer is the arbiter.

## WHO IS THE CONSUMER? ANSWERS FROM AD AGENCY ACCOUNT TEAMS

Marketing management is, in part, an exercise in social control, but it cannot compel or coerce, it must try to persuade, seduce, entice, to hector, or to tease[22] its way to a sale. In the absence of a universal bolt-on formula for successful marketing, practitioners effectively act as applied social scientists, trying one method after another to encourage the desired outcomes in a given context. One striking absence, though, from any marketing text books I have encountered, is a discussion of different models of the person. I don't mean "who is the consumer" in the sense of how the target segment is defined, but rather what sort of being is a consumer? As I indicated at the beginning of the chapter, the nature of the human within the human condition is a staple topic for any introduction to social science, yet in marketing courses and text books it seldom merits a mention. However, intuitive answers to the question of who, or what, is a consumer, implicitly underpin practice.

I tried to conceptualize just how important the model of the person can be in marketing practice in several research studies I conducted of advertising agency work. Ad agency work is normally done by account teams, consisting of an account manager, who manages client relations and directs the account team, an account planner who is responsible for research and strategy, and the creative team who think up the ad. I suggested that these three roles tend to work to different implicit models of the consumer. These differences in perspective give working in the advertising business its (creative) tension. I speculated that there were three pre-eminent, and implicit, models[23] that underpinned contributions to planning and strategy discussions.

Account management seemed to consider the consumer through a machine-metaphor, and this drove their thinking about strategy. The assumption was of a mechanistic relationship between input and output. Programme the right things into the consumer, and the desired behavior will result. The consumer is regarded implicitly as an entity that behaves unthinkingly according to external stimuli: a biological machine. The marketing task is to control the machine by ascertaining the correct input. This implicit model introduces a bias into the way many account managers think about research, planning, and creativity in advertising.

The account planners, in contrast, seemed to assume that the consumer is a meaning-seeking creature, with consciousness and imagination, and this implies that advertising must make a symbolic connection with the target audience. This assumption drives account planners' reasoning around advertising strategy. Advertising, they feel, must resonate with a sense of truth for the consumer, in order to generate an emotional response. Their implicit model of the consumer, then, regards the consumer as a seeker after meaning, and therefore advertising must supply that meaning in the form of communications that resonate with the consumers' subjective experience.

Thirdly, there are the creatives. They are the arty types dressed in jeans and boots, who feel that, actually, they are the most important people in the agency because they have the ideas, without which the agency has nothing to sell. The creatives, I suggested in the research, held to a third implicit model of the consumer. They saw consumers as distracted, impatient, and preoccupied beings who need to be activated with inspiring stories and images. For creatives, with an inclination toward art, aesthetics, and poetics, advertising is the commercial use of art. Art cannot move people emotionally through a purely physiological process, and it is not enough for it to reflect their own lives back at them. It must also move them with its beauty. For creatives, advertising, as popular art, is an expression of the sublime, made especially for the masses.

My implicit models of the consumer are crude stereotypes, but, as implicit biases in thinking, they do have implications for the kinds of marketing intervention that might be decided upon in response to a given brief. In day-to-day marketing practice, people do not have social scientific discussions about the assumptions underpinning their ideas, but that does not mean there are none. There are unarticulated theoretical assumptions built into every marketing strategy. Clearly, for example, a machine-metaphor model of the consumer is necessary to neuro-marketing, which assumes that human beings respond unthinkingly to brain stimulation. If the correct parts of the brain are stimulated by marketing stimuli, then the desired behavior will result. It's that simple, or is it? Truth is, neuropsychology is an infant discipline, and the brain displays a good deal of plasticity – the brain can adapt to use different parts for different functions. In addition, human beings are capable of reflexivity: we can reflect on our autonomous responses, and countermand them with our will. Just because my hippocampus might light up when I see an ad for a bag of potato chips doesn't necessarily mean I'm going to buy and eat them.

True, a Magnetic Resonance Imaging (MRI) scanner might highlight unconscious responses to stimuli such as a package design or advertisement, thereby by-passing the problem of rationalization in self-reports. Another problem with brain responses, though, is that there is no reason why responses could not be socially mediated. In other words, our emotions are culturally constructed, and in a naturalistic consuming situation, say, in a shop with some friends or watching TV with family, the emotional response could be shaped by the social context. Put me in a scanner and show me an ad, and one part of my grey matter might start flashing like a belisha beacon. Show me the same ad when I'm in the pub with friends, and a different part could light up. In fact, neuro-marketing research repeats a failing that has dogged advertising research for years, in that experimental situations fail to replicate the naturalistic social environment in which consumers consume. But don't tell that to the marketing director who just sunk ten years' research budget into a scanner and a team of graduate neuroscientists. There are more layers of theoretical assumptions than you might expect in the pragmatic, seat-of-the-pants, intuitive world of marketing practice, and the model of the consumer as a machine is one of the most common.

If, say, one prefers a model of the consumer as a meaning-seeking creature, like the account planner, then one would have to give ground to the possibility that consumers can reflect on, question, and, to a degree, become aware of our own responses to external stimuli. Being aware of these stimuli and their effect on us, we can adapt our behavior. If I buy a large bag of sweet popcorn at the cinema, I know from experience that I cannot stop eating the stuff until I've finished the whole bag. So, if I was concerned about my weight, I'd avoid buying it, or I'd buy a smaller bag. Cognitive stimuli have a range of operation, but humans are capable of rationalizing situations to decide how and where to engage with our environment. Neuro-marketing and its mechanistic model of the consumer reflects the marketers' dream of by-passing human self-reflection to achieve behavioral control. To be sure, a great deal of consumption is done on auto-pilot. We often consume without critical reflection. However, our consumer behavior may often be socially mediated, rather than internally driven by neuro-psychological mechanisms. The account planners' model of the consumer as a seeker after meaning assumes that the keys to marketing lie in the consumers' lived experience. We spend our lives trying to find meaning, and marketing gives powerful cultural meanings to everyday activities like washing my hair, driving my car, even chewing a piece of chewing gum. This implicit theory has less allure for marketers, because it doesn't promise control over the consumer. Instead, it positions marketing as a site of mutual communication between business and consumers, in which it is incumbent on the marketers to reach out to, and understand, the consumers in their cultural context. This is conceptually and practically more difficult than simply programming inputs into consumer-machines, so it is less popular.

The thinking that people bring to marketing planning reflects their intellectual background and experience. The account manager in an advertising agency often has a business background, perhaps an MBA, and has learned to think about problems in terms of controllable causes and effects. Their instinct is to solve a clear-cut problem with a definitive solution, and this informs their thinking about communication. I acknowledge this is a stereotype – most are far more flexible than this, but my suggestion is that there is an implicit *emphasis* in thinking, not that every case is reduced to a caricature. The account planner, on the other hand, often has a liberal arts or social science intellectual background and thinks about social life in a different way. For many of them, the connection a marketing communication has to make with a consumer is not physiological, or behavioral, but cultural and symbolic. Finally, creatives think in terms of art and aesthetics. Their perspective is that consumers need their mashed potato or their toilet tissue to activate and inspire them with images of beauty that will distract them from the dreary business of getting through the day. Like the shadows on the wall of Plato's cave, advertisements provide that distraction. I am being a little sardonic here, and I would not argue that there is a zero-sum game in which one position must win out in the battle for ownership of strategy. I am suggesting that the social scientific problem of human nature and agency is not avoided by business education because it isn't relevant to practice. It's avoided because it's difficult to conceptualize. Practitioners' strategic thinking is founded on their implicit theories of human nature, but business education has never grasped the need to incorporate this into curricula and research.

The three perspectives are not free-standing social theories but they arise partly out of the politics of ad agencies.[24] The account manager, for example, has the job of representing the client, while clients are often answerable to main boards consisting of professionals from many disciplines. The way their thinking shapes strategy discussions is influenced by the need to justify budget and strategy decisions to a wide range of different people. Input-output theories map onto hard scientific research data, and this kind of rationality is more acceptable to client representatives. Creatives, on the other hand, do not necessarily have to reflect the client's viewpoint. They may not even have to communicate with the client, so they are not faced with the problem of having to articulate and communicate their reasoning to a risk-averse client. However sophisticated clients may be, they really want to hear that their input is going to generate the desired output.

The context of negotiation and communication, then, can frame the kinds of discussion about strategic thinking that can take place.

## STRUCTURE, OR AGENCY?

So, when I buy a pair of cheap sports socks imprinted with a *Nike* swoosh logo from the *Sports Direct* discount retailer to wear at the gym, am I responding unconsciously to the color, the allure of the merchandising display, the subtly seductive store layout? Am I making a rational assessment of the utility of the socks and the relative price and quality of the fabric and weave in comparison to other brands? Or am I buying because wearing *Nike* taps into wider cultural myths about self and identity? These three alternatives by no means cover the whole panoply of buyer motivations, but they loosely reflect the three stereotypical models of the consumer that I outlined above. On the face of it, only the third, reflecting the account planner's implicit model of the consumer as an interpreting, meaning-seeking creature, allows consumers the capacity for self-reflective behavior. Clearly, that capacity would also be contingent on other elements of the consumer's cultural context, such as education level, age, social class, life experience and economic circumstances.

Of course, if we are to ask what is at work here, social structure, or autonomous consumer agency, the answer could be both, and neither. If I am influenced as a consumer by cognitive, physiological, or behavioral stimuli in the store, I am hardly exercising any agency. Similarly, if I buy my *Nike* socks because I subconsciously want to be part of the *Nike* crowd, I am not exactly a brand rebel either. On the other hand, I might have made an independent evaluation of the value and utility of the socks, or I could have made a conscious decision to wear *Nike* because all my friends wear *Puma*, which could mean that I am, after all, an agentive thinker, to an extent. I think the pragmatic answer for marketing practitioners is that the power of the individual to express discernment through consumption in the pursuit of identity strategies must be acknowledged. Equally, the practitioners must acknowledge that there is an essential social component to subjectivity. Our sense of individuality is realized in a social context. Brands can act as myths with which we can play identity games, resolve conflicts, and explore dilemmas. Structure and agency achieve a dialectical interplay through consumption.

There is nothing new about positing different levels of influence in marketing. In typical marketing buyer behavior models, though, these influences funnel into the buyer's decision-making process. In other words, the consumer is assumed to be sovereign over our own subjectivity. We buy according to our *decisions*, not our rationalizations, and not our unconscious, emotional impulses. The model, though, fails to recognize that our evaluations, whether explicit or not, do not take place in a cultural vacuum but are framed by wider ideologies. Our inner subjectivities are in dialogue with the wider world. There is a field of interplay between them within which we might exercise our sense of agency. The signification of the marketing mix elements operate within a wider sign-system, and what we imagine to be our decisions may not be as autonomous as we like to think.

Marketing, as a field that embraces the full context of consumer culture, can be conceived, then, as an applied arm of behavioral science. Its appeal to the basest instincts of greed and individualism gives it the purest integrity as a testing bed for behavioral interventions. Whatever people may feel about marketing, this is the sharp edge, and humans respond to marketing without coercion or compunction. We respond because we like it. When we are eating fatty fast food, drinking sugar-loaded drinks, voting for our favored political party, or choosing a new car or TV set, we may face the massive promotional resources of global corporations telling us what our happy lifestyle should look like, but in the end, we are free to choose. True, the choice might be delimited by concentrated market structures, but it is nonetheless a choice. Marketing gives us a rich resource of symbols with which we can play in our experimentation around identity, fantasy, authenticity, and sheer hedonism. But where does the subjective I, end, and the postmodern Me, begin? The sharp relief of the individual subject of marketing sometimes seems to fade into the landscape when the bigger mise-en-scéne perspective is considered. In marketing, as in the rest of social life, individuals are not necessarily quite as individual as we like to suppose.

A great deal of academic marketing research conceives of the consumer as an individual operating in a social vacuum. Hoards of marketing professors publish research in cognitive science journals, and most consumer behavior theory is conceived on a similarly individualistic model. This research tradition operates largely in a bubble, bracketed away from sociology, anthropology, and the other human sciences. It is hugely influential in dictating the path of many academic careers in university business schools, yet marketing practice is no nearer to having a scientific set of principles for behavioral control over consumers than it was 100 years ago when the first academic marketing research began. It is hard to see how it can, given that it makes a virtue of stripping out context from marketing behavior in favour of a spurious sense of control. We all have a unique biography and an equally unique reflexive sense of our selves, but our consuming behaviors are embedded in our cultural context. This is where behaviors are conceived and played out, and this is the realm in which marketing operates most effectively.

Consumption might sometimes be a site for the assertion of individualism and creativity, but it must be acknowledged that much of our consumer behavior is habitual and routine. Indeed, this is the key assumption of a cultural approach. Marketing, performed with careful attention to context, can insert particular consumption norms into the taken-for-granted habitus of everyday life for targeted groups. Some consumer purchases might be accounted for by cognitive factors, such as, say, a £9.99 price point. Others might have a behavioral explanation, like the impulse purchase of chewing gum displayed conveniently at a supermarket checkout. Still others have a cultural basis, such as the British unwillingness to drink cold tea or iced coffee. Lipton's lemon iced tea is gradually becoming available in more outlets the UK, but it is clearly a slow process to challenge the cultural norm in the UK that tea should be served hot, and with milk. Marketing demands an understanding of how different levels of explanation interact in particular cultural contexts.

The aphorism that culture eats strategy for breakfast is usually attributed to management writer Peter Drucker and refers to organizational rather than consumer culture. Marketing initiatives have to be imbued with a sense of meaning in order to resonate with consumers, and this aspect of marketing is cultural, rather than cognitive. Tattoos, for example, have become a mainstream consumer fashion and a huge consumer industry in the West, although they retain their transgressive connotations as marks of rebellion and statements of marginalization. They are distinctive marks of individualism, yet, like the *Puma* campaign discussed above, the individual achieves legitimacy through the group. A tattoo is a public communication, at least when exposed, and the individualism of particular tattoos is linked with the wider cultural currency of the tattoo as symbol of transgression. Group influence is powerful, but so is the subjective need to assert some sense of autonomy, to feel that one's individuality is authentic. Marketing exploits this tension by appealing to our individual need for social status and recognition, and it offers to resolve it by conferring a symbolic social status through display, of brands, body art, or other consumer cultural symbols. Tattooing and body art are examples of the bodily inculcation of consumption practices.

The bodily aspect of consumption is yet another area that receives relatively little attention in the marketing literature, yet commodities such as beer, hair shampoo, coffee sweetener, skin cream, hair dye, fake tan, and countless others intimately affect our subjective sense of self. The fad for fake tan amongst many girls in the UK is part of collective experience that adjusts the cultural standards of what is thought to be physically attractive, within some groups, if not others. Cognitive approaches to understanding marketing seem to fall short of accounting for the ways in which consumption practices subsist not in our heads, but in the social spaces between us. Our bodies offer an end point at which all marketing converges.

The potential of marketing techniques to manipulate our individual psychology has been overplayed since Vance Packard wrote his sensational exposé of marketing's use of depth psychology, *Hidden Persuaders*, more than 50 years ago. Marketing's operation as an ideological form of influence, though, is still little understood. Marketing activity operates most powerfully at a cultural level, cueing, and framing our beliefs, behaviors, and rationalizations and normalizing them within our consumer experiences. The contextual approach as both a mode of practice and a disciplinary perspective embraces the individual within the cultural, and engages creatively with the resulting tension.

# CHAPTER 7

# Managing Marketing – In Context

## CONVENTIONAL MARKETING AND CONTEXTUAL MARKETING

So far, I've tried to focus mainly on the ways in which a contextual approach brings out the detail and conditionality of particular marketing initiatives. I've tried to account for the different levels of context that operate in interaction, the cultural, social, and individual. In keeping with the style of books about marketing, I've made claims here and there about how this approach is new and improved, and altogether better than the old, tired, sad, "classic," analogue, steam-powered, marketing management ways. Of course, marketing has proved remarkably robust as a discourse of markets, management, and consumption for the past 30 years. As I've noted many times in this book, marketing's concepts and values have entered the popular lexicon of management and business, and beyond into public policy. This book isn't the place for an extended critique of marketing theory,[1] but it may be useful to try to draw out some distinctions between the ways of conceiving marketing that have proved so popular, and the contextual approach I've tried to set out here.

One part of marketing discourse that has proved especially popular has been its tendency to focus on abstract process categories without filling in the all-important detail of the link between these and the consumer insight. This technical style of marketing management discourse has proved hugely influential in consulting, education, publishing, and beyond, but its grounding in the experiential worlds of consumers and managers, and the linkages between cases, principles, and applications, frequently lacks that all-important specificity. Categories such as the Marketing Mix elements (the Four Ps of Price, Product, Promotion, and Physical distribution) supply a working vocabulary of marketing variables, but they are crude concepts for articulating the way marketing is grounded in everyday situations and practices,[2] and they seldom offer penetrating insights into marketing effects. For this level of detail, the mutual relativity of marketing effects *in their cultural context* has to be understood. So, rather than the four Ps, think of the 4 S's, for Systemic, Symbolic, Spontaneous, and Social. Or perhaps the 4 Cs: Connotative: Contingent: Creative, Contextual.

I see traditional marketing approaches in terms of a largely static, abstract, and hierarchical sequence of analysis, planning, implementation, and control (first popularized by Professor Philip Kotler some 45 years ago[3]) which lacks meaning without a situational context to give substance to the abstractions. It must be admitted, though, that the sheer contingency of marketing practice is a hard sell for a management book. Practitioners know well enough that every marketing situation is uniquely different, and management gurus sell counter-intuitive panaceas that eventually turn out to have been counter intuitive for a reason. They work best on the printed page or in the lecture hall. Over the years, Marketing has proved most effective at selling one thing: itself. There is a big demand for boil-in-the-bag management solutions. Part of this demand is the tendency for simplistic marketing solutions to echo prevailing values of neo-liberal ideology, and hence fit with organizational agenda. The powerful ideological role of marketing talk and writing as a disciplining discourse means that the lack of efficacy of text book marketing solutions is often overlooked. Marketing doesn't work the way the text books claim, yet the text books don't change, at least, not all that much. They are plausible and accessible, yet they lack penetration into the complexity of marketing practice in a convergent economy.

Conceding that, actually, there is no easy formula for marketing management does not necessarily mean that we have to give up on marketing as a subject of research, scholarship, and management education. The idea that the most effective marketing solutions and strategies are grounded in an insightful appreciation of the cultural context may be no more than a truism. Nonetheless, it can be a point of departure for a more critically self-reflective and intellectually nuanced marketing discipline. Marketing practice is an area where informal social science, street anthropology, and practical experience meet. Marketing is a process that entails seeking insight and understanding into people in their socio-cultural context. In this way I see continuity between an inclusive and eclectic marketing education, and a reflexive and creative marketing practice.

## MEDIA BRANDS AND MARKETING

The contextual approach highlights the power of marketing to create long term, strategic advantage from ostensibly, short term, tactical action. Getting a brand placed in a TV show or movie might be considered a tactical maneuver of minor import, unless it's *Heineken* spending dozens of millions of dollars on placement in *Skyfall*, with tie-ins.[4] When *Coca Cola* decided to ship free bottles of product to US servicemen abroad during WW2 in what would be categorized as a tactical maneuver, they probably didn't imagine that they were building a cultural myth around *Coke* and its identification with America that would fuel the *Coke* brand for years to come.[5] Some of the examples of ad hoc, spontaneous marketing initiatives I've referred to in this book have resulted in levels of exposure that would, as part of a planned strategy, cost many millions. Astute, contextually informed marketing, can have a profound strategic effect. Part of my argument in the book is that marketing can be far more valuable, and more "strategic," than conventional business thinking concedes, provided it is not conceived as a set of universal techniques but as a pragmatic and context – dependent discipline.

As part of my argument for a broadened scope of marketing, I referred to some media brands as exemplars of contextual marketing that can be especially illustrative, since they sit at the nexus of the convergence economy. There are two main levels of convergence. One is technical, as the software and hardware are developed that will eventually allow us to access all digital media on one device. The other is textual, as media genres such as news and entertainment converge. In both, marketing is central to the effect. In conventional marketing thinking, communication is conceived as an afterthought, a means of conveying the marketing message to targeted consumers. I maintain that the communication should not be an afterthought but, rather, is a constituent part of the offer. As such, communication is far more central to marketing than the conventional hierarchy of marketing sub-disciplines concedes. As I've noted before, what is a market but a forum for communication?

For example, the fading UK TV franchise *X Factor* has developed multiple revenue streams and opportunities for brand engagement off its TV platform. These include its lucrative telephone voting system, the opportunity for fans to buy and download music releases and live show tickets through the website, the ways the website can leverage product placement and sponsorship in the TV show, the advertising the website carries to take advantage of the massive audience traffic, and the cross-promotion of other ITV shows, and of artists managed by Simon Cowell's companies. The viewing figures may be falling away, but *X Factor* set new standards in integrated media brand marketing. Another striking media brand is the *Daily Mail* newspaper's online operation, *MailOnline*. The *Daily Mail* has the second highest circulation of any national print newspaper in the UK,[6] at just under 2 million, but circulations, and revenues, are dropping for all print media. Most major newspapers are experimenting with digital formats in order to try to develop new business models to offset the shift of readers to digital. The *Daily Mail* has done this with remarkable success. The sixth biggest news site in the world, and the biggest newspaper website with 111 million unique users per month,[7] *MailOnline* generated £3.4 million in digital advertising revenue in March 2013 and expects to make £45 million over the year.[8] Digital revenues are rising at over 30% on the year and 43% of the visits are accessed on mobile devices. This contrasts with the revenue from the print newspaper, which is healthy by print newspaper standards at some £650 million last year, but is in a declining trajectory. The *MailOnline* expects its digital revenue to overtake its print revenues in just 2 or 3 years.

The *Daily Mail*'s brand positioning may be popular but it is also controversial. It is perceived by some as having an ideologically driven stance of sensationalized "bad" news stories, focusing on such topics as "binge" drinkers, teenage mothers, welfare scroungers, celebrity gossip and scandal, sexual crime, and immigration. The ideal *Mail* story might be about an obese, binge-drinking asylum-seeker who refuses to work but claims child benefit for 14 children, had cosmetic surgery on the NHS, and lives on welfare in a mansion in Hampstead, paid for with state housing benefit. *The Mail* is regularly vilified by some UK media commentators for harassing people in the pursuit of stories and for poor fact-checking, as well as for selling a sensationalized, bad news-driven, right-wing world-view. Setting aside such cavils, the stunning success of the *MailOnline* is ineluctably a marketing triumph. Typically for media brands, there is no sense of having asked consumers what they want, as the classic marketing orthodoxy might suggest. This is cultural leadership on a Fordist model, notwithstanding the fact that it is a kind of leadership that some dislike. The truth is, the *MailOnline* has taken a conceptual leap in moving away from the idea that it is a digital version of the print newspaper, and operates as an entirely different beast according to the rules of digital, not print. For example, its print constituency of middle class, white British, middle-aged female readers is quite different to its digital reader profile, which is far broader, and global in scope. The *MailOnline* adapts its content internationally – for example, accessing the site from the US generates a mix of mainly US stories. The homepage is packed with scores of well-constructed, if often prurient, stories, colorfully illustrated and broken up with several levels of sub-heading. Most importantly, the stories are updated constantly, with new ones every half hour or so. User engagement is assisted by an easy-to-use system for readers to join in the spleen by leaving comments. Many of the stories rhetorically invite outraged or sympathetic responses, and many readers are happy to oblige, often with opinions that are as fatuous as the stories, but with inferior spelling. It's all a thoroughly entertaining riot of overwrought tittle-tattle and sensation, and it generates deeper engagement than any of its rivals because readers stay on the page for upwards of 40 minutes, and return regularly. The banner advertising is used sparingly, and seems less intrusive than, say, Facebook advertising, which annoyingly interrupts the newsfeed. In addition to the more sensational or prurient coverage, the *MailOnline* carries some well-researched and informative stories about historical or cultural issues, along with occasional right-wing polemics. The mix of coverage, though, shouldn't distract from the key element – a commitment to the story arc, above all.

In a climate of rapidly declining reader engagement with news media, many newspapers are moving to "paywall" websites that charge visitors to read the content, with limited success. Others are simply hemorrhaging money as their advertising revenue disappears, along with their paying readers. The *MailOnline* produces comprehensive 24/7 news-ertainment coverage, free to access, and written in an engaging if rather florid style. It has shifted the concept of news coverage to fit a wider cultural shift away from objectivity, reflecting the shift to an entertainment economy.[9] Readers are clearly engaged, or perhaps enraged, with the "news as entertainment" positioning. It has broadened the notion of a newspaper brand and sees its competitors not only as the *New York Times* and other great newspapers, but also the likes of *MSN* and *Google News*. It's a ruthless game cleverly played, and it turns on an astute understanding of the cultural shifts in news and media consumption. *MailOnline* has successfully morphed news and entertainment, and its success owes little to conventional marketing principles. It is an enterprise in popular journalism that exploits high levels of literacy, a desire for a rapid turnover of well-presented, lively stories, and an appetite for self-righteousness, both from the political right, and from the left. Its success might be depressing for those who lament the way populist media have come to distort public debate on policy and politics, but it is a case study in giving consumers what they enjoy, free of charge, and still making a huge profit. Put this way, the success of *MailOnline* seems about as counterintuitive a case of marketing success as you can get. The cultural and technological context of news consumption has changed, and *MailOnline* has responded to these changes astutely.

## PHILOSOPHICAL ASSUMPTIONS IN MARKETING MANAGEMENT

So, in the preceding pages I've tried to make a case that business, and also the non-profit, professional services and charities sectors, could improve their marketing by making the effort to understand the contexts of marketing and consumption. I've used the analogy of the mise-en-scéne to try to illustrate the way that I feel the most interesting marketing operates, and to move away from the simplistic, cue-ball causality of cognitive marketing theories and input-output models of marketing practice. Through the mise-en-scéne analogy I also want to show marketing in a creative light, as a communication-oriented enterprise that engages and activates consumers, but does not compel, control, or, indeed, "satisfy" them. The ways in which consumers interpret their cultural mises-en-scéne are open and contingent. The most interesting marketing has, perhaps, always been about engagement, in some form, but this aspect of the discipline is especially evident in the new, media-dominated economy.

I'm by no means the only person to point out that the efficacy of marketing strategies is culturally contingent. For example, a brand agency's survey lists the top brands for their "cultural traction," based on their VIBE (Visionary, Inspirational, Bold, Exciting). Google was top in 2013,[10] but *Samsung* was third, closing fast on *Apple*. The survey claims that brand equity measures the current monetary value of a brand, but VIBE measures its future value as a cultural currency. Other management and marketing books have, in different ways, made compelling cases for the need for brands to be understood as socially constructed, cultural products. There are many different ways of conceiving this, though, and much scope for misunderstanding. In particular, these ideas often fall victim to an instinctive reification, a tendency to treat abstract concepts, as material things.

Culture, for example, is often conceived as an entity composed of fixed attitudes and behaviors, rather than as a dynamic process. In other words, "culture" is conceived as a material thing, when it has no qualities of thing-ness. My use of the word in this book assumes that culture refers to the self-generating and self-sustaining flow of what people do, including what we say and think. In other words, culture is a process. In this usage the term culture is not loaded with implications of "high" culture: it refers broadly to the practices we undertake to make our world more meaningful. Culture isn't something "out there," as a static independent variable for marketers to exploit. For some, taking account of "culture" means you have to make sure the brand name doesn't mean anything rude in the native language. Culture is often seen as a set of stereotypical behaviors and attitudes (note the frequent use of "national" culture stereotypes in cross-cultural management[11]) that constitute a barrier to be overcome, rather than a process to be assimilated into strategic thinking.

Another quasi-philosophical assumption common in management theory is the assumption that cognition and culture are mutually exclusive. In other words, what I think, is ontologically independent of the world around me. As discussed in the previous chapter, the relationship between human agency and social structure can be considered as a two-way dialectic, rather than a dichotomy. The ideas we internalize came from that world around us, so culture and cognition can be thought of as a continuum, each inter-penetrating the other. Our thinking styles, emotions, attitudes, and beliefs, and the myths we live by, arise not in our heads, but in the wider culture of which we are part. That doesn't imply that we are no more than mimicking creatures – rather, we are creative curators, we assimilate language, myths, and ideas, and assemble them in ways that we feel express our subjective selves. I'm not forgetting that this is a book about marketing, and not a treatise on human nature. I'm just drawing attention to the futility of consumer behavior theories that close off any questions around the nature of human being and thinking, in favour of a poorly specified model of a consumer as a machine. Marketing is about people and culture, yet marketing management textbooks and courses tends to eschew a considered analysis of either.

The notion of agency is seldom addressed in management education, and this leads to much conceptual confusion in consumer behavior theory. A one-dimensional, cardboard cut-out model of the consumer strips out the complexities and contradictions of the human experience, but it also leaves the models adrift of the social life they purport to explain and predict. For example, consumers are often represented either as autonomous and rational "decision" makers, as in the AIDA model of persuasive communication,[12] or as unthinking automatons, as in, say, neuromarketing, regardless of the context. In academic marketing research, experimental studies strip out the cultural context from consumption, and position the consumer as an autonomous actor operating in a cultural vacuum. The results of experimental studies can be intriguing, and they might stimulate new strategy directions. There are many fascinating experiments on consumer attention, perception, recall, and attitudes. However, the experimental context seldom has ecological validity. It fails to capture the cultural context of consumer behavior, and creates artificial laboratory situations because they are easier to control and measure. Most forms of consumption are socially mediated events, and they don't take place in an experimental booth.

In advertising, the creative execution, the key idea for the ad, is often tested experimentally before the client will agree to sign off on the campaign. The ad will be portrayed in animation or through storyboards, to gauge response from a panel of consumers. The panel watch the ad on a computer screen in a "link test" and then respond to a questionnaire. Creative professionals hate this kind of "copy testing" research, partly because they just want their ideas to be made, but partly also because the research does not re-create how an ad is actually viewed in a naturally occurring consumer environment. Copy-testing has the added disadvantage that the sample of consumers used in the research does not accurately represent the target audience.

The implicit assumptions brought to strategy discussions about human agency carry another frequent, and rarely examined assumption. This is that human qualities, such as memory and attitudes, are universal, rather than cultural. This tendency to universalize is a problem that underpins much cognitive science, not to mention social science. It leaks into thinking in management very easily since management education seldom engages critically with broader questions of the philosophy of social science. Conceptual schemes tend to be imported into marketing and management studies and cut adrift from their original theoretical context. Management panaceas gain such popular currency precisely because they exploit the lack of philosophical and social scientific building blocks in management thinking and education. One normative management solution after the other sweeps the worlds of consulting and how-to management books. These solutions, arising through a particular context, gain such currency that they are then applied in new contexts. They fail, because their efficacy was contingent on the original context, and the cycle continues.

Another philosophical deficit in management and business thinking is the tendency to gloss over what philosophers call the "is-ought" problem. This is the assumption that normative, "how-to" conclusions can logically follow from positive, fact-based premises.[13] Marketing, above all, the other management sub-fields, has become closely associated with a naive normative style, consisting in prescriptions for action that are based on little more than evidence-lite assertions about the world. Writers of marketing books cannot solve marketing problems, since books cannot assimilate the particulars of situated action. A book provides a space for reflection on the processes by which those problems might be addressed. The normative enterprise in marketing and other how-to management approaches is founded on a logical fallacy.

## MORE THOUGHTS ON THE CONSUMER CULTURAL MISE-EN-SCÉNE

The metaphor of the mise-en-scéne is not just a fancy way of positing a sort of cultural placement, whereby the brand is inserted into the consumer habitus,[14] to take its place in the familiar, embodied, everyday experiential world of consumer routine. It is also meant to convey the magic that happens when a theatre director demonstrates the subtle grasp of audience psychology that is needed to create an emotional mood, to give dramatic substance to a line or a character, or to bring a sense of history and import to the action, merely through the spatial and auditory arrangement of the scene. To do this requires a deep understanding of the social milieu of the audience, as well as experience in the effects of different mises-en-scéne. Seeing the marketing manager as a theatre director might stretch the imagination somewhat, given that most peoples' image of a marketing manager is more akin to a down-at-heel car salesman. It would be fair comment to point out that most day-to-day marketing practice involves pragmatic tasks with a short-term outcome – most marketing professionals are not designing the set, but working in front-of-house, trying to get the audience into the seats, or perhaps bring them ice cream. Nonetheless, I think the contextual perspective can benefit not only big, strategic thinking in marketing, but also the short term, pragmatic activities. Several of the examples I've described in the book, such as the *Dr Dre* and *Bodyform* examples, span both categories, as pragmatic, short-term initiatives that have potentially longer term, strategic implications.

I've acknowledged that a weakness of the theatre metaphor is that consumers are not just a static audience, sitting in their seats watching the marketing performance, as it were, but that we are often mobile. As consumers we can move through one mise-en-scéne after another, the movement bringing a relativistic complexity to the calculation of stage arrangement and audience effects. I watch TV in my living room and review my social media and online newspapers on my mobile phone as I eat my breakfast. I see OOH advertising, vehicular advertising, promotional leaflets, and classified ads on my commute through the busy streets. If I go to a football match in the evening, I might move from the sponsored lounge area to the pitch-side seating with its view of plasma screen advertising around the field of play. I can buy sales promotional items in the club shop, drink out of branded cups, buy sponsored merchandise. Marketing is part of a consumer universe in which settings move through each other, as we move between them. Sometimes, the movement is merely implied, and that is all that is needed. A promotion for breakfast cereal *Weetabix*, for example, enabled children to download a game involving the *Weetakid* character from the brand website, to play on their mobile devices. The brand might be familiar to kids from visits to the supermarket, or it might not, in which case it would just seem like a nice, free game. But the game cannot be mastered without energy boosts for *Weetakid*, and the only way to get the energy boosts is to use the mobile device to scan a QR code on a box of the breakfast cereal. So, the free-to-download game accessed children playing web-based games on their iPads at home, but then spanned the physical distance to the supermarket, where the cereal boxes carrying the promotion had to be bought. The promotion was designed to get kids who didn't eat *Weetabix* to ask their Mum or other responsible adult to buy it. The promotion was banned by the UK regulator[15] for exploiting children, but it does conjure up a marketing world in which an advergaming promotion that refers inter-textually to a supermarket can be played by a child sitting in a car that is moving through urban settings, furnished with Out Of Home billboards.[16]

The mise-en-scéne metaphor, then, has its limitations. There are mises-en-scéne (or mise-en-scénes) within mises-en-scéne. As consumers move there is a mutually relatively perspective that is difficult for marketers to capture. But I think the metaphor also has a useful flexibility. It asks the marketer to consider the place of the marketing intervention within the context of the wider physical and cultural environment that surrounds the consumers. It allows, in principle, for the mobility of audiences as they move through consumer culture. It also allows the audience a range of interpretive possibilities. The design of the mise-en-scéne is crafted with an effect in mind, but the effect must be achieved by the audience and cannot be imposed hegemonically upon it in a way that is beyond resistance or reinterpretation. True, there are plenty of movies, stage plays, or other media content that can be accused of being exploitative and/or propagandistic. My point is, that even these achieve their effect through the way they manipulate the audience's process of interpretation. They do not, and cannot, impose any ideology that the audience do not bring to their interpretation. Many modern movies, directed by people who learned their trade in adver-tising, use rapid cutting and close-ups to try to tell the story by directing the viewer's attention. This might be satisfactory for passive viewers, but it reflects a lack of confidence both in the story to be told, and in the audience's imagination.

Even some marketing entities that are regarded as highly directive, perhaps propagandistic, in the approach, work best by leaving some scope for resistance. The *MailOnline* website, for example, discussed earlier, carries reader comment threads that sometimes contain criticism of the story or the journalism that produced it. The comments offer a full range of reader responses, from the readers who react exactly as primed by the article[17] (a "hegemonic" reading, in literary theory), to those who point to the absurdity of the reasoning or evidence in the story. Through the metaphor of the mise-en-scéne, marketing is constituted as an art that not only leaves space for consumers to resist or reject, as well as acquiesce, but it cannot operate without that space. In other words, while marketing's influence might not necessarily be benign, it is not merely a crude science of consumer control. Perhaps it would like to be, but the most powerful marketing is both less clever than that, and more subtle.

## THEORY AND PRACTICE IN CONTEXTUAL MARKETING

In support of my views on the role of contextual under-standing in effective and creative marketing practice, I've invoked some esoteric snippets of theory to hint at a number of intellectual traditions that I feel are relevant. These include some long-established ideas from cultural and critical studies, but applied well beyond their usual disciplinary field. This risks annoying everybody, because the practitioners might find it all over-intellectualized, and the academics might find it just…well, wrong. I contend, though, that although expert practitioners in marketing do not use theory in their strategic reasoning, it does not mean that their reasoning lacks an implicit theoretical sophistication. While theory is important, theoretical terms often carry baggage which can inflect the discussion with implicit assumptions. This is why I feel that the non-technical language expert marketing practitioners use to articulate their working experiences is worthy of remark.

As a generalization, the popular business vocabulary of management books rests on implicit assumptions that the world of consumption is static, concrete, and objective, reflecting what social scientists call a realist ontology of the world. The expert practitioners that have most impressed me talk about strategic issues of marketing and communication in ordinary language. They tend to avoid technical marketing terms, and use an implicitly relativist ontology of the world. They do not adopt this approach from a carefully thought-through philosophy, but as a working assumption which allows them the conceptual space they need to evaluate strategy as it unfolds in practice. In this way, expert practitioners use language that reflects the fluidity of the marketing context and the contingency of marketing interventions.

I've touched on some central problems of social science, because they are also the central problems of marketing. Marketing and management have evolved in parallel with the social sciences, but also set apart from them. One consequence of this separation is that management and business studies as a field is insulated from the internecine squabbles of more integrated disciplines. Marketing, as sub-field of management and business studies, is a huge academic and publishing enterprise. There are countless sub-sub fields within it, each working to their own agenda, rather than to the agenda of the informing disciplines. For many purists in the informing disciplines of sociology, anthropology, econometrics, and so on, this de-legitimizes marketing as an intellectual enterprise. The application of theory to marketing is seen as a superficial and self-referential exercise, and it is unusual for research conducted by marketing and consumer research academics that applies theories from cognitive science, anthropology, or sociology to be cited in the main disciplinary journals. I'd like to think that the engagement with business and policy practice can have an enabling effect too. Business and policy are vast empirical testing beds for social scientific ideas, and ideas can be adapted and applied to social situations without the burden of intra-disciplinary rivalries and prejudices. For example, psychoanalytic ideas have been deployed in organizational studies of management team dynamics and decision making, when some psychology departments have banned Freud from the curriculum because of a prevailing intellectual prejudice in some schools of psychology against psychodynamic theory. Marketing academics who apply ideas from anthropology, for their part, can ignore the internecine bitterness that has riven anthropology recently over the kinds of question I've touched on above, concerning the relative influence of social structure and human agency, because they can publish their research in management journals.

There are other negative aspects to business studies' magpie approach to social science. Business and management is notorious for its selective use of theory, and marketing, in particular, has a habit of taking theoretical tit bits from sociology and psychology out of their original context, and mis-applying them in a crude pursuit of managerial relevance.[18] One of my favorite bugbears in this respect concerns the way humanistic psychologist Abraham Maslow's hierarchy of needs is used in marketing text books to justify a materialistic lifestyle. Self-realization through consumption is hardly what Maslow had in mind for his humanistic psychology, and the widespread use of his ideas in marketing is a deeply cynical mis-application of those ideas.

I've focused a discussion on the context of marketing, as a significant subset of management and policy action, to try to make two points. Practical thinking is laden with rudimentary, everyday theory: implicit theory, if you will. There is just no getting away from it, and the many management books that claim to eschew theory in favour of a discussion of practical management "reality," are making an impossible claim. "Theory" means different things to different people, and this isn't the place for that discussion. But, the subjective experience of management practice can only be represented in a book: representation is one thing, and practice another. Conflating the two distinct realms of books about management on the one hand, and management practice, on the other, is a useful rhetorical device for management polemicists who want to distract the reader from the intellectual poverty of their account of management practice.[19] It represents a deep ontological confusion that is common throughout academic management and business studies.

Not only is theory central to marketing, and management, practice, but it needn't be as scary as you might think. Pre-school kids are able to grasp basic philosophical concepts, if they're explained well. Management writing, though, usually avoids questions of the philosophy of social science. Issues of causation, the nature of the social world, the nature of identity, the interplay of social structure and human agency, the nature of knowledge, and the answer to the question of what is the Good Life, are the ghosts in the marketing machine. A broadened consideration of social scientific theory for marketing practice seems all the more important, given the broadened scope of the discipline. Marketing is now charged with major policy initiatives as a tool of (putatively benign) civic persuasion. I've deliberately mentioned some policy examples as well as commercial ones because marketing, as a way of thinking and talking about markets and management, has insinuated itself deeply into public policy arenas. Marketing isn't just a marginal academic subject to be studied by ambitious individualists for their self-serving ends: it has become widely used in government-sponsored "social" marketing campaigns, and a necessary part of the charities and non-profit sectors. Marketing is invoked by national governments and local public authorities in the promotion of policy ends and better citizenship. Recently in the UK there have even fashionably ironic government TV advertising campaigns portraying sexual battery, in the belief that these will be taken by young people as non-patronizing warnings of the morally bankrupt nature of such behavior. I have my doubts – normalization can have a powerfully de-sensitizing effect, and the irony may be lost on the target audience. In other words, there is a real risk that such portrayals of reprehensible behavior might have the unintended consequence of dampening the moral outrage with which it is viewed. The application of marketing logic to policy contexts is often lacking in a contextual understanding.

Marketing is sometimes seen as a tool promoting social equality when, for example, state-sponsored campaigns promote the availability of state benefits or educational opportunities, or when they attempt to address demographically skewed health inequalities by encouraging people to eat more healthily or to give up smoking. There is a potential contradiction in the use of marketing techniques, like advertising campaigns, to promote social equality, because they also superficially mask social inequality, through branding. Overall, the use of marketing in policy is just another reason why more people need to understand marketing better, in order to engage critically with it from a well-informed basis.

## MARKETING AND POWER

This book is conceived as a practice-focused and not a sociological analysis. It commits many theoretical errors of oversimplification and conflation. I am about to commit another, since I want to refer to power in marketing, touched upon earlier in the discussion about market structures. The single-minded pursuit, in academic marketing research, of a cognitive science of consumer control, is not only wasteful, but wholly inadequate as an intellectual enterprise because it lacks a theorization of power in consumer cultural contexts. Marketing is not only limited but also enabled by its managerial remit, since the practical issues of how organizations engage with consumption cultures provide rich empirical settings for exploring just how ideologies and cultural influence play out in particular cases. Power runs through the constitution of marketing management interventions, as it does through other social exchanges.

Marketing power comes in various forms. For example, drugs, software, or minerals companies might hold a powerful market position through, say, control over an element of the supply chain, ownership of intellectual property, of raw materials, or of technology. Dominant market positions can be maintained through buying up patents that might generate competition, by vertical takeovers, by cost control and economies of scale, or by setting marketing and new product development expenditure at a level that few others can match. A consideration of the play of power in constituting marketing relationships is fundamental to understanding how supply chains and markets work. Structural or "hard" power can be conceived as that which can be enforced directly, for example by legal enforcement of intellectual property or control of supply. Constitutive or "soft" power might be thought of as the power to influence thinking so that people internalize values and relations and regard them as taken-for-granted, say, through PR, press lobbying or advertising. Those same big companies that enjoy the structural market power also enjoy the biggest budgets for PR, advertising, and lobbying, so they also benefit from constitutive power by influencing communication channels. Companies such as Google, Apple and Microsoft are great organizations with an acute sense of the context of their operations, and they have all been accused of anti-competitive practices at one time or another. Successful marketing organizations understand the politics and power of markets and competition.

Of course, end users have an order of power as well. If the market is competitive enough to have substitutes, then consumers can exercise power collectively through choice, notwithstanding the possibility that those choices have already been framed by marketing interventions. Within supply chains, buyers can exercise considerable individual power. UK supermarkets, for example, have attained such a scale within an oligopolistic market that they can ruthlessly suppress supplier prices. UK farmers have complained bitterly that they sell milk to supermarkets at barely above cost, because the supermarkets control the price. Back in the consumer market, in addition to our economic power of choice, we consumers have some access to constitutive power if we have access to social media. We can talk about brands and consumer experiences; we can share emails and videos. Sometimes, we can contribute to a groundswell of opinion that forces a corporation to respond, and perhaps to change its policy. The power that web "2.0" confers on consumers, though, can be just as overstated as the power of corporations to dominate economic life. But what cannot be doubted is marketing studies typically lacks the conceptual vocabulary to express one of the most obvious things about economic life – namely, that it is a site where power plays out.

I feel that the cases I've chosen show that this power is not necessarily hegemonic and dominant: it can be resisted, subverted, and adapted. We can be individuals, within our groups or communities. The power marketing wields is culturally negotiated, and as consumers and citizens we are often complicit in the power we accede to marketing, even though it may not suit us to believe that. It is easier to set marketing apart as an influence upon us, rather than to concede that we often get the marketing we deserve.

I think a critical understanding of marketing power is important not only for consumers, citizens, policy makers, and intellectuals, but also for practitioners. Marketing, as a field of academic courses and textbooks, has become an ideological vehicle that fiercely resists critical interrogation, but in this form it serves only academics and consultants, and the politicians whose agenda is driven by myths about markets. I think it is hard to argue from any political stand-point that economic efficiency and social welfare would not be better served by a more critically penetrating understanding of marketing processes. Better organizational marketing, and more critically informed and active consumers, are in everyone's interest.

## MARKETING AND MANAGERIALISM

In addition to a consideration of power, a sense of proportion is important in marketing, and I hope this proportionality is another contribution of the contextual approach. There are many intellectual fields which offer insights into marketing but which are marginalized into silos of critical or consumer studies and hived off from the typical MBA curriculum because of the way that simplistic, case-based normative thinking dominates over critical thinking in the field. Marketing textbooks are often over-eager to rush to a bolt-on, "how-to" conclusion that promises to make the reader a successful practitioner. There is an impulse to appear managerially relevant, but this often results in the managerial task being caricatured, in order to fit formulaic solutions. Marketing is too important to be studied so superficially, and fair consideration needs to be taken of theoretical explanation. The normative approach to marketing, the excitable how-to genre of books and courses, exploits students' naiveté about marketing practice, and glosses over the contradictions and paradoxes that should be the foci of marketing analysis and education.

Marketing covers a host of phenomena that have potentially wide societal implications, and these need to be contemplated in a sociological spirit. The impulse to rush to managerial implications needs to be deferred in favour of a cooler appraisal. The adjective "managerial" in academic business studies sometimes applies to an ideologically driven, but intellectually superficial, pro-business emphasis that positions the student as a quasi-managerial "decision-maker," but eschews a careful consideration of context. Part of the role of business studies is indeed to try to encourage a commercial problem-solving mentality – it is, after all, an applied discipline. Management books and courses are expected to have a normative, "how-to" element, but a sense of proportion[20] is needed too, to avoid the recourse to a simplistic, case-based reasoning. In the end, academic books and courses can do only one thing – apply and impart the principles of scholarship and intellectual analysis, with the aim of nurturing students' better judgment. Managers cannot be trained in a classroom, but they can be educated.

Finally, the contextual approach reflects the most impressive thinking and organization I've seen in marketing practice. I've found strategy discussion at this level to be deeply nuanced and contingent. It eschews marketing clichés and simplistic cause-effect assumptions and considers the socio-cultural consumer context in a spirit of pragmatism and openness. The experiential reasoning behind astute marketing strategy is leavened with implicit theoretical positions. Academic management books have a role in trying to articulate these implicit assumptions, since they are an intrinsic part of the most astute commercial reasoning. There is a need for a theory of practice in marketing. The thinking around marketing expertise is still an enigma, and much remains to be done to understand the way commercial awareness and marketing creativity are acquired and exercised. This is not merely a matter of "cognitive styles," which may be habitual but are also contingent, like personality traits. There is a great deal of research on the psychology of expertise, but this line of research cannot define a cognitive ability in a complex field that constantly presents practitioners with uniquely particular challenges. Cognitive ability is exercised in its application, and that application needs experience to improve, whether you're a bricklayer, a footballer, a chess player, or indeed a marketing manager.[21] Being commercially smart in marketing doesn't require any management books or academic learning: practical expertise can be acquired with experience alone. A very long line of creative entrepreneurs in marketing bears testimony to this truism. Academics and management writers have a role, though, in trying to delineate the components of successful strategic thinking in management, with the goal of improving management practice, education and policy, and of enhancing the cultural understanding of this most important and influential field. This book makes the case, then, that the best thinking in marketing takes in the consumer cultural contexts of marketing and consumption.

## CONTEXTUAL THINKING IN MARKETING PRACTICE

Marketing interventions that are informed by an acute organizational sensitivity to the socio-cultural context of consumption cannot be reduced to a formula. The main characteristic of the approach is creativity, informed by and integrated with, consumer insights. It seems to me, though, that there are organizational traits that may be consistent with the contextual approach. For example, there is a particular kind of organization that seems to be able to engage with context, and that is an organization where ideas and people are valued so that open discussion takes place within an informal, yet clearly demarcated, hierarchy. Contextual marketing usually requires cross-functional collaboration: joined-up thinking, in other words, and that implies that the human capital in these organizations is valued. Organizations need the right kinds of people in order to be able to function with the relatively flat structures and informal climate that open strategy debate demands. The personal qualities of the best strategic thinkers include intrinsic motivation, commitment to the work, astute social and communication skills, and intellect. There has to be a climate that is receptive to ideas and enables voices to be heard, but this cannot be a cacophony of opinion. Participants need the social sensitivity to express ideas at an appropriate time in the input, and to make them worth hearing. That means being passionate about the work but also emotionally poised, and having good self-editing skills. Points have to be expressed succinctly by managers, unlike academics. There is also a need for acute listening skills. Contextual marketing ideas need to be interrogated rigorously and developed iteratively, so individuals need to be able to assimilate others' critique into their own ideas, or to concede when another's point is stronger. This means listening skills, an integral aspect of communication skill. Finally, there is a need for rhetorical skills, but not in a pulpit-pounding sense. So much of marketing consists in the use of language, that sensitivity to its persuasive techniques, sensitivity to rhetoric, is indispensible for marketing professionals who wish to influence strategy and policy.

So, there seem to be a number of broad preconditions for contextual marketing strategy to emerge in an organizational setting. There is a need for an organizational climate that facilitates the creative discussion of ideas. This carries an implication about recruitment, because people have to be able to work in this way with intensity and also with emotional containment. These are not common abilities. In addition to personal (and inter-personal) skills and abilities, there is a need for an intellect. Marketing is a knowledge-based industry and various differing knowledges that contribute to strategic thinking have to be assimilated by strategic thinkers. These might include conceptual knowledge of market and consumer research, of consumer culture, and communication, and also knowledge of production and communication technology, engineering processes, and/or service contexts. Most importantly, to offset the risk that free, creative exchange of ideas becomes chaotic, the organization needs a set of informal and flexible, but clearly understood and internalized working methods. The informal hierarchy must be clearly understood, because creative discussions need leadership. In the end, someone has to decide when an idea gets a green light, and it is important that the leadership role is founded on respect for achievements and personal characteristics. Explicitly authoritarian management styles would not sit comfortably with an ethos of collegial ideas-sharing. Collaborative teams in a knowledge-based industry such as marketing need to ensure that ideas are given a fair hearing, because if people feel that their voice has been rejected unfairly, they may be less willing to participate fully in the next project, and potentially valuable ideas could be withheld or blocked. On that point, professional marketers do have to be emotionally robust when ideas are countermanded or rejected. It is a tough and unforgiving environment, and the politics can be subtle but ruthless.

An organization's capability at implementing a contextual marketing approach, then, depends a great deal on the creativity, social skills, intellectual poise, and communication skills of its people. An implication of this is that marketing education should not focus only on abstract, technical processes, and superficial case applications, but on developing critical intellectual judgment. The mise-en-scéne analogy suggests that the most striking marketing practice applies creative interventions in settings that are fluid and unpredictable. The kinds of people who can do this will draw fluidly on eclectic, multi-disciplinary understanding of art, aesthetics, and consumer cultures, as well as quantitative and technical skills.

I have suggested that research in marketing is often used as a blunt instrument, and fulfils a sensitive political role in organizations as well as an important role in generating consumer insights and market knowledge. Research is useful only if it is interpreted with sensitivity to the nuance of social data. Research data do not speak for themselves, and skills of interpreting research are in short supply. "Research" is a powerful word, and research methods are often used as rhetorical devices to persuade the impressionable. "Research has found" can be a useful term to use before saying something preposterously under-evidenced. Research findings often invoke both credulity and cynicism, but research, nonetheless, has an indispensible role in marketing. Marketers need to form judgments for managerial action that are founded on knowledge and insight about unfamiliar worlds. Research, carefully crafted and interpreted, is capable of teasing out nuanced insights about the consumer cultural contexts of marketing that can inform strategy. The question becomes, what kind of research is fit for particular purposes?

Communicating research insights to others in the team is a potential source of tension and difficulty. The team members may not share a common vocabulary of research under-standing if they have differing educational backgrounds. It is important, then, for contextual marketing practitioners to have a broad conceptual grasp of research approaches, even if they don't necessarily have detailed knowledge of specific methods. It is important to be able to understand broadly what a research study can tell you, and what it cannot. Research in business is invariably a mere snapshot of a consumer or market phenomenon, whatever the method or sample size. It does not offer proof of suppositions, it cannot predict the future, and it doesn't tell people what they should do. What it can do, though, is to bring plausible truths, insights, or material facts into the discussion, and these can shift the strategic perspective and open up new possibilities for action.

Marketing practice often entails science, in, say, advanced production technology, in the use of logarithms for directing web browsing, in techniques of data mining and so on, but marketing practice is not scientific. The elimination of human judgment from marketing strategy is really not advisable.[22] A great deal of research in business mimics natural science, but fails the tests of natural science. There is a need for empirical facts to be gathered, about consumers and markets. There is also a need for marketing professionals to gain a sense of what a particular brand or consumption practice means to a given group of consumers in a specific cultural context. The contextual approach invites a particular stance on research, because of the world-view it implies. The kind of research most appropriate to contextual marketing operates in a discovery mode, and takes a provisional, tentative view of the nature of social life. Contextual marketing research seeks to understand how consumers make their lives meaningful, and the role brands and consumption play in this process. The goal is to generate an insight upon which a marketing intervention can turn. This implies that contextual marketing research is often best carried out through the selective inter-pretation of qualitative research data sets, such as interviews, discussion (or "focus") groups, observation, consumer diaries, or internet data sets[23] produced by consumers, about consumption.

Implementation of contextual marketing strategies builds on the elements discussed above: collaborative, multi-perspectival analysis, and astute and insightful use of research-derived information. Implementation also demands the flexibility to put strategies into action without recourse to a many-layered bureaucracy. Throughout the book I've delib-erately used case examples that are creative, rapidly executed, well co-ordinated, and communication oriented, because they seem, to me, to epitomize the way marketing has moved in the convergence economy. The contextual approach flows with the pulse of consumer culture, and must, therefore, operate according to its rhythms. Five- or ten-year strategic plans might be useful as organizational devices for instilling a sense of unity and purpose, but they don't fit with the quick-silver world of marketing in its cultural context. This is the biggest challenge for marketing, since it often lacks a strategic presence in organizations, despite its strategic importance. As a consequence of marketing's ambivalent status as a cultural product, it can lack the weight of authority within organiza-tions to influence strategies and policies that demand a cross-functional operation where, say, product design needs to be co-ordinated with marketing, advertising, and branding.

My aim in this book has been to try to show that an appre-ciation of context illuminates the marketing process. I have not tried to set out a join-the-dots action plan for marketing effectiveness. There are already too many of these, and they represent marketing management as a tick-box, mechanistic process, rather than a creative one. Marketing initiatives that dovetail with consumer cultural context are often striking and creative, and they sometimes spring from a world-view that turns business orthodoxy on its head. Contextual marketing insights reflect marketing's place as a site of cultural tension, in which dialectical oppositions play out, between structure and agency, and domination and resistance. Marketing sets the scene for contemporary consumer cultural life. Organizations, citizens, and wider society can benefit from a deeper understanding of the techniques and processes through which the marketing we get comes about. The mises-en-scéne of contemporary life are the theatres of consumer culture in an age in which media technologies dominate our lives. With this analogy I have tried to convey the creative and aesthetic character of much of the most compelling marketing practice. I have also tried to show that marketing is not a neutral, technical, and mechanistic process of human domination, but a field in which values are important. Consumers should not be conceived as means, but as participants and partners in the production of marketing and brands.

# Notes

## 1 Setting the marketing scene

1. For more on this topic see C. Hackley (2003) "'We Are All Customers Now': Rhetorical Strategy and Ideological Control in Marketing Management Texts," *Journal of Management Studies* 40(5), 1325–1352. Another excellent source is S. Brown (2005) *Writing Marketing*, London, Sage.
2. For example, see B. Ardley (2005) "Marketing Managers and Their Life World: Explorations in Strategic Planning Using the Phenomenological Interview," *The Marketing Review*, 5(2), 111–127. ISSN: 1472–1384.
3. For more on implicit theories in advertising management see A. J. Kover (1995) "Copywriters' Implicit Theories of Communication: An Exploration," *Journal of Consumer Research*, 21, March, 598–611, or C. Hackley (2003) "How Divergent Beliefs Cause Account Team Conflict", *International Journal of Advertising*, 22(3), 313–332.
4. I've tried to describe my understanding of account planning in several academic papers, including C. Hackley (2003) "Account Planning: Current Agency Perspectives on An Advertising Enigma", *Journal of Advertising Research* 43(2), 235–246. Two of the more authoritative accounts include S. Pollitt (1979) "How I Started Account Planning in Agencies." *Campaign,* April 20, and J. Steel (1988) *Truth, Lies and Advertising: The Art of Account Planning.* New York, Wiley.
5. I became familiar with the term through work done by my former student, Marco Nappolini, with whom I wrote a working paper about product placement in movies that can be accessed at http://digirep.rhul.ac.uk/items/5765dcaa-e5d1-4351-d3c6-b649127880a3/5/ (accessed 8.5.2013). I've stretched the flexibility of the metaphor to suit a wider purpose in using it to express the way marketing shapes

consumer environments and frames consumption choices. Since writing this book I've become aware of one or two marketing companies who use the term, though not in the sweeping way that I do.

6. See, in particular, T. Adorno (1991), *The Culture Industry*, ed. J.M. Bernstein, London, Routledge, for the view that mass culture is exploitative and formulaic, and lacks the quality that high art has to activate aesthetic and moral responses in audiences.

7. My estimate is 1 million, expressed in several earlier books (e.g., C. Hackley (2009) *Marketing: A Critical Introduction*, London, Sage) and based on an estimate of students taking trade examinations including *Chartered Institute of Marketing*, CAM, *Institute of Direct Marketing* and many more, plus the huge success of university business and management degrees in which marketing constitutes a major or minor subject.

8. R. H. Thaler and C. R. Sunstein (2008) *Nudge: Improving Decisions About Health, Wealth, and Happiness*, New Haven and London, Yale University Press.

9. See http://www.bartleboglehegarty.com/#!/global/aboutus/history (accessed 2.3.2013).

10. My colleague Alan Bradshaw has written of the role of popular music in consumer culture. Here is his lucid review of *The Sounds of Capitalism: Advertising, Music and the Conquest of Culture* by T. D. Taylor, published by University of Chicago Press http://royalhollowaymarketing.blogspot.co.uk/2013/03/review-of-sounds-ofcapitalism.html (accessed 2.3.2013).

11. There are lots of versions of *Laundrette* uploaded to YouTube; this is one of them http://www.youtube.com/watch?v=u06rDf-kUt0 (accessed 2.3.2013).

12. C. Hackley (2009) "Parallel Universes and Disciplinary Space: The Bifurcation of Managerialism and Social Science in Marketing Studies", *Journal of Marketing Management* 25(7–8), 643–659.

13. I got interested in the tacit aspects of marketing practice quite a while ago, and tried to theorize it in this paper: C. Hackley (1999) "Tacit Knowledge and the Epistemology

of Expertise in Strategic Marketing Management" *European Journal of Marketing*, Special Edition: Marketing Pedagogy, 33(7–8), 720–735.

14. This is called source credibility in advertising.
15. I've written an outline of the development of advertising theory in C. Hackley (2010) "Theorizing Advertising: Managerial, Scientific and Cultural Approaches," chapter 6 in P. MacLaran, M. Saren, B. Stern, and M. Tadajewski (eds) *The Sage Handbook of Marketing Theory*, London, Sage, pp. 89–107.
16. V. Packard (1957), *The Hidden Persuaders*, New York, Washington Square Press..
17. For academic perspectives on the politics of marketing science see, for example, M. Tadajewski (2008) "Incommensurable Paradigms, Cognitive Bias and the Politics of Marketing Theory," *Marketing Theory*, September 8, 273–297. Tadajewski has also written in the same journal about the history of phrenology in marketing: "Character Analysis and Racism in Marketing Theory and Practice," *Marketing Theory*, December 2012, 12(4), 485–508.

## 2   Marketing as communication

1. For example, see Wired, http://www.techdirt.com/articles/20130203/21125221870/oreo-wins-superbowl-ad-wars-with-timely-tweet.shtml (accessed 22.02.2013).
2. http://newsfeed.time.com/2013/02/04/watch-oreos-snappy-super-bowl-blackout-ad/ (accessed 5.02.2013).
3. http://online.wsj.com/article/SB10001424127887324900204578282360008085752.html (accessed 5.02.2013).
4. For a detailed analysis of Dichter's work in historical context see M. Tadajewski (2006) "Remembering Motivation Research: Toward An Alternative Genealogy of Interpretive 'Consumer Research,'" *Marketing Theory* 6(4), 429–466, full copy at http://www.uk.sagepub.com/ellis/SO%20Readings/Chapter%201%20-%20Tadajewski.pdf (accessed 4.3.2013).
5. See http://usatoday30.usatoday.com/life/television/news/nielsens-charts.htm (accessed 10.4.2013).

6. See Robert Kozinets on netnography http://kozinets.net/ (accessed 9.5.2013).

7. I've also discussed this case in my advertising textbook, but the piece isn't merely cribbed, honest – I take a different angle on it here: see C. Hackley (2010) *Advertising and Promotion: An Integrated Marketing Communications Approach*, London, Sage.

8. This is a comment often attributed to a *Revlon* executive and used in textbooks as an illustration of the way the marketing concept focuses on end-user benefit. Other similar illustrations include the alleged comment of a power tools executive that "We don't sell drills, we sell holes."

9. http://www.dove.co.uk/en/Our-Mission/Self-Esteem-Toolkit-and-Resources/default.aspx (accessed 4.3.2013).

10. http://www.youtube.com/watch?v=iYhCn0jf46U (accessed 22.02.2013).

11. This comment is based on nothing more scientific than my discussion with students while teaching in Hong Kong, and my observation of the poster advertising for the brand.

12. *Dove* "Thought Before Action" viral video http://www.youtube.com/watch?v=m0JF4QxPpvM (accessed 7.3.2013).

13. Quo Vadis blog, http://www.qvbrands.com/dove-rant/ (accessed 7.3.2013).

14. This Huffington Post comment was one of hundreds, http://www.huffingtonpost.co.uk/2012/06/21/women-femfresh-vagina-outrage_n_1616156.html (accessed 22.02.2013). This was another http://jezebel.com/5920297/intimate-hygiene-product-ad-is-scared-of-the-word-vagina (accessed 22.02.2013).

15. http://www.guardian.co.uk/world/2012/jun/15/michigan-politician-banned-using-word-vagina (accessed 22.02.2013).

16. The post is here https://www.facebook.com/Bodyform/posts/10151186887359324 (accessed 23.02.2013).

17. *Bodyform*'s video response is here: http://www.youtube.com/watch?v=Bpy75q2DDow (accessed 23.02.2013).

18. Including this piece in the UK *Daily Mail* http://www.dailymail.co.uk/femail/article-2218920/Bodyform-viral-spoof-

YouTube-video-Response-Richard-Neills-Facebook-rant-period-adverts.html (accessed 23.02.2013).

19. I've written more about this in, for example, C. Hackley (2010) "Theorizing Advertising: Managerial, Scientific and Cultural Approaches," chapter 6 in P. MacLaran, M. Saren, B. Stern and M. Tadajewski (eds) *The Sage Handbook of Marketing Theory*, London, Sage, pp. 89–107.

20. See previous note for more on AIDA.

21. For the BBC News account of the story see http://news.bbc.co.uk/1/hi/uk/1222326.stm (accessed 4.3.2013).

22. The collection of Adorno's essays, *The Culture Industry*, referenced in Chapter 1, sets out a view of popular culture as a dismal, formulaic, and repetitive tool that sedates and controls the masses in the interests of capitalism. The idea of a postmodern culture industry acknowledges the vaguely unified interests behind mass media (which now include social media) but resists the view that pop culture lacks the ability of high art and culture to engage and elevate the human spirit with creativity. In Chapter 4 I touch on Guy Debord's notion of the Spectacle of mediated capitalism, another slant on the Culture Industry thesis.

23. Fast Moving Consumer Goods.

24. For more on this topic, please see C. Hackley (2009) *Marketing: A Critical Introduction*, London, Sage.

25. See, for example, P. Svensson (2004), *Setting the Marketing Scene: Reality Production in Everyday Marketing Work*, PhD Thesis, Lund Business School Press http://www.lu.se/lup/publication/21565 (accessed 10.4.2013). Also see B. Ardley (2009) *a Phenomenological Perspective on the Work of the Marketing Manager: An Analysis of the Process of Strategic Planning in Organisations*, Lambert Academic Publishing.

26. My Advertising text book has more on this topic, referenced in the previous chapter. Academic journal articles include, for example, C. Hackley (2003) "Account Planning: Current Agency Perspectives on An Advertising Enigma," *Journal of Advertising Research* 43(2), 235–246. This and several others on account planning in advertising can be read in pre-print on my Royal Holloway research pages

http://pure.rhul.ac.uk/portal/en/persons/christopher-hack-ley_bb78fbaf-7641–4f8f-87c0–57dc1b4db16f.html or my academia.edu pages http://royalholloway.academia.edu/ChrisHackley/Papers

27. Notably Stephen Brown www.sfxbrown.com

28. For an entertaining and informative diatribe against the marketing concept see S. Brown (2003) *Free Gift Inside*, Chichester, UK, Capstone.

29. Late historian Roland Marchand has written of the ad agencies' role in legitimizing big business in *Creating the Corporate Soul: The Rise of Public Relations and Corporate Imagery in American Big Business* (1998), University of California Press. His more famous book, also dealing with the influence of ad agencies in framing consumer culture, is *Advertising the American Dream- Making Way for Modernity* (1992), University of California Press.

## 3  Marketing ideology and mass media

1. For a review of the role of Andrew Wernick's idea of promotional culture, see H. Powell (ed.) (2013) *Promotional Culture and Convergence*, London, Sage, available at http://www.amazon.co.uk/Promotional-Culture-Convergence-Markets-Methods/dp/0415672805/ref=sr_1_sc_1?ie=UTF8&qid=1368105577&sr=8–1-spell&keywords=promotional+cultuire+and+convergence

2. One of Bernays's many initiatives involved the promotion of eating bacon, and he got a large number of medical experts to endorse its value as part of a healthy breakfast. It is thought that the iconic culinary status of bacon in the USA today owes much to Bernays's PR on its behalf.

3. See the IMDB website for the full quote http://www.imdb.com/title/tt0458352/quotes (accessed 28.02.2013).

4. See, for a recent paper on this process, B. K. Loo, and C. Hackley (2013) "Internationalisation Strategy of Iconic Malaysian High Fashion Brands," *Qualitative Market Research: An International Journal* 16(4), 406–420.

5. Marxist literary theorists Terry Eagleton has written much on ideology, e.g. T. Eagleton (2007) *Ideology: An Introduction*, London, Verso.
6. I discuss this in Chapter 7.
7. So taken am I by this show, I led a Saturday evening "research project" that resulted in a journal paper: C. Hackley, S. Brown, and R. A. Hackley (2012) "The X Factor Enigma: Simon Cowell and the Marketization of Existential Liminality," *Marketing Theory*, 12(4), 451–469.
8. I genuinely enjoy the show, and I'd audition with my guitar, if I was braver. I'm a fan of open mic formats and talent shows, and I auditioned for the *X Factor* of the 1970s, *Opportunity Knocks*. I failed the audition, and became a professor instead.
9. For my take on "content marketing" see my blogpiece http://www.chris-hackley.com/2013/05/marketing-and-media-content-new-frontier.html (accessed 9.5.2013).
10. I know, "parasitic" doesn't even begin to cover this, but, in my defense, I'd claim that my role in this marketing-media machine is one of keen amateur. I'm fascinated by the way publicity works. Our *X Factor* research (later published in *Marketing Theory*) was the topic of several media features, for example this one in *Advertising Age* in October 2011, http://adage.com/article/global-news/understanding-x-factor-simon-cowell-arch-shaman/230402/, (accessed 6.3.2013), along with lots of shorter references in the national press, such as this one in the *Guardian's* media supplement http://www.guardian.co.uk/media/mediamonkeyblog/2011/oct/13/simon-cowell-high-priest-x-factor (accessed 6.3.2013).
11. My academic interest in the show resulted in a moment of liminality for me too. During a radio interview about our research in which I tried and hopelessly failed to explain our theory in everyday language, I was declared the first professor of *X Factor* by a popular radio host. It is my personal tragedy that I was proud enough of this to put the clip on *YouTube*: http://www.youtube.com/watch?v=uvK0EazWlLg (accessed 6.3.2013). This is far from being my only venture

into the quicksands of media exposure. Another one that illustrated the currency of propaganda theories of media concerned an opinion article I wrote for the UK university academics' trade magazine, *Times Higher* (aka THES). The article expressed my concern at a school education reform proposed by the UK Government's Education Secretary. In my innocence, I didn't see it as a party political issue at all, but the Education Secretary's paid assistants (known as SPADS – special advisors) went to the trouble of trolling me online over the issue. The whole story is here on my blog http://www.chris-hackley.com/2013/02/w.html (accessed 6.3.2013) and the original article that caused the fuss, with the online comments is here http://www.timeshighereducation.co.uk/story.asp?sectioncode=26&storycode=422594&c=1 (accessed 6.3.2013). The argument was then picked up by *Private Eye* magazine (Eye 1334, February 21, 2013, p. 8) giving me my other Proudest Moment.

12. Please see my comment on Adorno's term in the notes for the previous chapter. Adorno did seem to take the view that popular culture had no merit at all other than as a tool of capitalism, which seems a little one-dimensional to me. You decide: T. W. Adorno (2001) *The Culture Industry: Selected Essays on Mass Culture*, Ed. J.M. Bernstein, London, Routledge.

13. You can see the *Coca Cola* content marketing strategy here http://www.youtube.com/watch?v=LerdMmWjU_E&feature=youtu.be (accessed 28.02.2013). Part two of the video is here http://www.youtube.com/watch?v=fiwIq-8GWA8.

14. See the story and the movies here http://twistedsifter.com/2009/08/bmw-films-the-hire/ (accessed 6.3.2013).

15. See the story, and the movie in *Advertising Age* http://adage.com/article/news/jaguar-s-12-minute-film-starring-homeland-s-damian-lewis/241063/ (accessed 9.5.2013).

16. For more on TV product placement as branded content see C. Hackley and Hackley née R. A. Tiwsakul (2012) "Unpaid Product Placement: The Elephant in the Room in the UK's New Paid-For Product Placement Market," *International Journal of Advertising*, 31(4), 703–718.

17. See D. Holt (2004) *How Brands Become Icons: The Principles of Cultural Branding*, Harvard Business Press.
18. See another of our papers on product placement, R. Tiwsakul and C. Hackley (2009) "The Meanings of 'Kod-sa-na-faeng' – Young Adults' Experiences of Television Product Placement in the UK and Thailand," in A. L. McGill and S. Shavitt (eds), *Advances in Consumer Research*, Vol. 36 Duluth, MN, Association for Consumer Research, pp. 584–586.
19. *T-Mobile* "Dance" flash mob on YouTube http://www.youtube.com/watch?v=VQ3d3KigPQM (accessed 7.3.2013).
20. V. Packard (1957) *The Hidden Persuaders*, Ig Publishing (reissue 2007).
21. E. Herman and N. Chomsky (1988), *Manufacturing Consent – The Political Economy of the Mass Media*, Pantheon.
22. 2.7 million was a circulation figure reported on some media sites in early 2012 e.g., http://www.thedrum.com/news/2012/02/10/circulation-gains-sun-daily-mirror-daily-star-and-daily-record-january-2012 (accessed 6.3.2013).
23. A. Ehrenberg, N. Barnard, R. Kennedy, and H. Bloom (2002), "Brand Advertising as Creative Publicity," *Journal of Advertising Research*, 42(4), 7–18.
24. J. Williamson (1994) *Decoding Advertisements*, Marion Boyars publishers.
25. W. Leiss, S. Kline, S. Jhally, and J. Botterill (2005) *Social Communication in Advertising; Consumption in the Mediated Marketplace* (3rd edn), Abingdon, Oxfordshire, Routledge, Taylor & Francis.
26. My Amazon review of Liz McFall's book is here: http://www.amazon.com/Advertising-Cultural-Economy-Representation-Identity/dp/0761942556 (accessed 7.3.2013).
27. There are other arguments about the lineage of visual representations of St Nicholas/Santa Claus, some drawing on the green man of English mythology, which I cannot arbitrate. My point here is just that Coke adapted and popularized one version of the image, identifying it with their brand.

28. Marcel Danesi has written some accessible and readable works on the semiotics of advertising – his general introduction to semiotics is *Of Cigarettes, High Heels, And Other Interesting Things: An Introduction to Semiotics (Semaphores and Signs)* (1999, 2nd edn 2008), New York, Palgrave Macmillan. I attempted a short introduction to advertising semiotics myself, some time ago in C. Hackley (1999) "The Communications Process and the Semiotic Boundary," chapter 9 in P.J. Kitchen (ed.) *Marketing Communications, Principles and Practice*, London, International Thomson, pp. 135–155. Umberto Eco wrote a much longer, and better one (1978) *A Theory of Semiotics*, 2nd edn, John Wiley.

29. It is, I confess, a long time I read up on semiotics, but I think this phrase came from work by J. Umiker-Sebeok (1987) *Marketing and Semiotics: New Directions in the Study of Signs for Sale (Approaches to Semiotics)*, Mouton de Gruyter.

30. I have discussed this in the context of an introductory treatment of other theories of advertising interpretation in this book chapter that is available on the web http://www.sagepub.com/upm-data/32952_02_Hackley_2e_CH_02.pdf (accessed 7.3.2013).

31. G. Cook (2002) *The Discourse of Advertising*, London, Routledge.

32. See G. McCracken (2005) *Culture and Consumption 11: Markets, Meaning and Brand Management*, Indiana University Press.

33. S. O'Donohoe (1997) "Raiding the Postmodern Pantry: Advertising Intertextuality and the Young Adult Audience," *European Journal of Marketing*, 31(3/4), 234–253.

34. One of the Frizzell ads can be seen on YouTube http://www.youtube.com/watch?v=I-e8Wr4xXuw (accessed 7.3.2013).

35. I gather that the plural for mise-en-scéne can be either mises-en-scéne or mise-en-scénes. If you know better, please just humor me, don't write in.

## 4  Ideologies of space

1. See for example J. F. Sherry Jr (1991) *Servicescapes – The Concept of Place in Contemporary Markets*, Chicago, NTC Business Books, and S. Brown and J. F. Sherry Jr (eds) (2003) *Time, Space and the Market: Retroscapes Rising*, M.E. Sharpe. The term was popularized by B. H. Booms and M.J. Bitner (1981). "Marketing Strategies and Organisation Structures for Service Firms," in J. Donnelly; W. R. George (eds), *Marketing of Services*. Chicago, American Marketing Association.
2. Some photographs of Sao Paulo's un-promotional visual culture here http://www.thelondonvandal.com/2013/01/sao-paulo-six-years-after-outdoor-advertising-ban/ (accessed 8.3.2013).
3. See note 21 in Chapter 2.
4. I wrote a guest blog piece on the topic of treating alcohol as a grocery product for an alcohol lobby group, available here: http://www.alcoholpolicy.net/2012/01/opinion-the-grocer-isation-of-alcohol-brands-and-the-contradictions-of-alcohol-policy-in-the-uk-.html (accessed 10.5.2013).
5. I discussed the British propensity for getting roaring drunk with some experts in alcohol and drug addiction in a BBC Radio 4 show called *Thinking Allowed* – the details are here and the podcast might still be available http://www.bbc.co.uk/programmes/b01pg54j (accessed 11.04.2013).
6. I was so moved by my latest *BMW* purchase I wrote an epistle to it on my blog: http://www.chris-hackley.com/2012/02/my-liminal-limousine.html.
7. For a far more authoritative and detailed exposition on this general theme see A. Wernick (1991) *Promotional Culture: Advertising, Ideology and Symbolic Expression*, London, Sage.
8. For an outline of the Unhate story see my blog piece http://www.chris-hackley.com/2011/11/why-benettons-unhate-campaign-gets-it.html (accessed 9.3.2013).
9. http://www.bicestervillage.com/en/company/about-us(accessed 8.3.2013).

10. http://library.nothingness.org/articles/SI/ (accessed 10.3.2013).
11. I have engaged in some more whimsical reflection on the Bicester Village phenomenon in a blog piece http://www.chris-hackley.com/2011/12/psychogeographical-ruminations-on.html (accessed 9.3.2013).
12. M. Coverley (2006), *Psychogeography*, Herfordshire, Pocket Essentials.
13. See C. Hackley, A. Bengry-Howell, C. Griffin, W. Mistral, and I. Szmigin (2011) "Young Peoples' Binge Drinking Constituted as a Deficit of Individual Self-Control in UK Government Alcohol Policy," chapter 15 in C. N. Candlin and J. Crichton (eds) *Discourses of Deficit*, Palgrave Macmillan, Hampshire, *Palgrave Studies in Professional and Organizational Discourse*, pp. 293–310.
14. I'm thinking here of some of Georges Bataille's work and his use of the anthropological concept of potlatch, where the more one gives the greater the social prestige and status implied. In the societies Bataille studied, individuals would sometimes ruin themselves by giving away everything they had, seemingly as a gesture of self-aggrandisement.
15. Some examples of academic studies of space and consumption here: http://www.marketingsemiotics.com/wp-content/uploads/2012/03/SpaceAndPlaceAbstract.pdf; http://www.ephemeraweb.org/journal/3-2/3-2styhreandengberg.pdf; http://www.ashgate.com/pdf/SamplePages/Consuming_Space_Intro.pdf all (accessed 10.3.2013).
16. See, for an example of the anthropological perspective on symbolic goods and identity, R. W. Belk (1988) "Possessions and the Extended Self," *Journal of Consumer Research*, 15(2), 139–68.

## 5  Marketing ideology and social policy

1. For the view that sociologies of advertising have neglected the material practices of the field see L. McFall (2004) *Advertising: A Cultural Economy*, London, Sage.

2. See C. Hackley (2009) *Marketing: A Critical Introduction*, London, Sage, for an introduction to some of the scholarship in this area.
3. Including visual rhetoric: J. E. Schroeder (2002) *Visual Consumption*, London, Routledge.
4. I outlined my view of marketing education as a critical and liberal intellectual enterprise in a short magazine piece called "Return on Investment" in the UK universities' trade magazine, the *Times Higher* or *THES*. I've linked it here http://www.timeshighereducation.co.uk/story.asp?sectionc ode=26&storycode=422477 (accessed 24.02.2013).
5. There are many other examples in R. H. Thaler and C. R. Sunstein (2008) *Nudge: Improving Decisions About Health, Wealth, and Happiness*, New Haven and London, Yale University Press..
6. Research by my former PhD student Dr Norman Peng described the adoption of political marketing by the UK Labour Party: N. Peng and C. Hackley (2007) "Political Marketing Communications Planning in the uk and Taiwan – Comparative Insights from Leading Practitioners," *Marketing Intelligence and Planning*, 25(5), 483–498.
7. See for reference a BBC news story, http://www.bbc.co.uk/ news/uk-13589976 (accessed 12.3.2013).
8. This estimate was reported in a BBC news story, http://news. bbc.co.uk/1/hi/health/3121440.stm (accessed 12.3.2013).
9. A BBC news article outlines the perceived failure of the ban on HFSS food advertising in children's TV programming, http://www.bbc.co.uk/news/uk-scotland-17414707 (accessed 14.3.2013).
10. The research was led by Professor Christine Griffin, with myself, Professor Isabelle Szmigin, and Dr Willm Mistral, helped by Dr Andrew Bengry-Howell: a summary of the Economic and Social Research Council funded study is here: http://www.academia.edu/2742714/Branded_con- sumption_and_social_identification_Young_people_and_ alcohol
11. A section of one of the ads is shown during a TV interview I did about it at the time – you can see a shaky YouTube

clip of the interview here: http://www.youtube.com/ watch?v=ZvpyoFiHBDo (accessed 15.03.2013).

12. See C. Griffin, A. Bengry-Howell, C. Hackley, W. Mistral, and I. Szmigin (2009) "'Every Time i Do It i Absolutely Annihilate Myself': Loss of (Self)-Consciousness and Loss of Memory in Young People's Drinking Narratives," *Sociology* 43(3), 457–477. Also see C. Hackley, A. Bengry-Howell, C. Griffin, W. Mistral, I. Szmigin, and Hackley née R. A. Tiwsakul (2012) "Young Adults and 'Binge' Drinking: A Bakhtinian Analysis," *Journal of Marketing Management*. DOI: 10.1080/0267257X.2012.729074 and I. Szmigin, A. Bengry-Howell, C. Griffin, C. Hackley, and W. Mistral (2011) "Social Marketing, Individual Responsibility and the 'Culture of Intoxication'," *European Journal of Marketing*, 45(5), 759–779.

13. The Institute of Alcohol Studies published this account of our point about the anti-drinking campaign, and *Diageo*'s response:http://www.ias.org.uk/resources/publications/alcohol-alert/alert200801/al200801_p6.html (accessed 14.3.2013). The issue was originally covered by national UK media, for example the BBC http://news.bbc.co.uk/1/hi/health/7132749. stm (accessed 14.3.2013).

14. This was an interview I gave on BBC Radio Five Live on December 11, 2007. I cannot remember the name of the show.

15. Alcoholic liver disease in the under thirties is said to have increased by 50% in a decade. One press report from 2011 here http://www.dailymail.co.uk/health/article-1350302/ Number-30s-liver-disease-soars-50-decade.html (accessed 15.3.2013).

16. I have a few examples of questions from creative briefs in my 2010 book *Advertising and Promotion: An Integrated Marketing Communications Approach* (2nd edn), London, Sage.

17. See, for example, http://www.alcohol-focus-scotland.org. uk/alcohol-and-marketing (accessed 14.3.2013).

18. See for an account of the contretemps C. Hackley (2008) UK Alcohol Policy and Market Research: Media Debates and Methodological Differences' "Viewpoint" article,

*International Journal of Market Research* 50(4), 429– 431, https://www.mrs.org.uk/ijmr_article/article/88173 (accessed 8.9.2013).

19. Our paper about the transgressive pleasures of intoxication is here http://www.tandfonline.com/doi/full/10.1080/026 7257X.2012.729074%20 and talked about it BBC Radio 4's Thinking Allowed hosted by Laurie Taylor, with Fiona Measham and James Mills, special edition on the pleasures of intoxication broadcast 4PM December 26, 2012 http://www.bbc.co.uk/programmes/b01pg54j podcast here http://castroller.com/podcasts/ThinkingAllowed/3272717 (accessed 14.3.2013).

20. When UK TV advertising was banned for cigarettes in 1965 the brands turned to posters. In famous campaigns for *Silk Cut* cigarettes, the advertising appeal of smoothness and mildness were abandoned for visual metaphors based on images of silk, and scissors cutting. This minimalist visual style became a well-understood shorthand for the brand that was reproduced in different forms across differing platforms.

21. German magazine *Der Speigel* carried a 2007 piece discussing the links between German companies and the Nazi regime http://www.spiegel.de/international/germany/break-ing-the-silence-bmw-s-quandt-family-to-investigate-wealth-amassed-in-third-reich-a-511193.html (accessed 16.3.2013).

22. I tell the story of this regulatory conundrum on my blog here: http://www.chris-hackley.com/2012/09/should-implied-meaning-in.html (accessed 16.03.2013).

23. S. J. Levy (1959), "Symbols for Sale," *Harvard Business Review* (July–August), 117–124.

24. For an overview see E. Arnould and C. Thompson (2005) "Consumer Culture Theory (CCT): Twenty Years of Research," *Journal of Consumer Research*, 31, 868–882.

## 6   Consumer agency and brand culture

1. I gleaned these corporate structures from a cursory glance around the internet, including this helpful blog: http://www.

socialphy.com/posts/off-topic/11574/The-10-Companies-
that-Control-Your-Consumption.html that, in turn, claimed
its source as another blog called Convergence Alimentaire
(accessed 17.3.2013).

2. http://www.kitkat.com/about.html (accessed 17.3.2013).
3. The takeover remains controversial locally in 2013
   http://www.yorkpress.co.uk/news/9571691.Call_for_
   Government_to_release_papers_concerning_Nestl_____s_
   takeover_of_Rowntree/ (accessed 17.03.2013).
4. For comment on the dominance of brand culture see, for
   example, N. Klein (2000) *No Logo*. London, Flamingo; R.
   V. Kozinets (2002) "Can Consumers Escape the Market?
   Emancipatory Illuminations from Burning Man," *Journal of
   Consumer Research*, 29, 20–39; J. E. Schroeder and M. Salzer-
   Morling (eds) (2005) *Brand Culture*, London, Routledge.
5. See, for example, B. Cova, R. V. Kozinets, and
   A. Shankar (2007) *Consumer Tribes*, Oxford, Butterworth-
   Heinemann.
6. See D. Bassiouni and C. Hackley (2011) "Do Generation
   Z Understand Brands Differently?," *7th Global Brand
   Conference, Academy of Marketing SIG, Said Business
   School University of Oxford*. This work is derived from Dr
   Bassiouni's PhD, awarded from Royal Holloway University
   of London, in 2013.
7. *Puma* competition "Worn My Way" campaign http://www.
   wornmyway.com/ (accessed 18.3.2013).
8. As reported in Brandrepublic http://www.brandrepublic.
   com/news/1174729/puma-seeks-celebrate-individuality-
   worn-lifestyle-campaign/ (accessed 18.3.2013).
9. http://adage.com/article/news/timberlake-beyonce-market-
   ing-titles/239712/ (accessed 18.3.2013).
10. See R. Barthes (1957) *Mythologies* (2010, trans. R. Howard),
    Hill and Wang.
11. A. Fuat Firat, and A. Venkatesh (1995) Liberatory
    Postmodernism and the Reenchantment of Consumption,
    *Journal of Consumer Research*, 22(3), 239–267.
12. I wrote a guest post for Alcohol Policy UK on the
    "Grocerisation" of alcohol – a term that was suggested to

me by John Snow after I'd been interviewed on Channel 4 News. The blog post is here: http://www.alcoholpolicy. net/2012/01/opinion-the-grocer-isation-of-alcohol-brands-and-the-contradictions-of-alcohol-policy-in-the-uk-.html (accessed 18.3.2013) and the clip of the Channel 4 interview is here on the ITN news site: http://www.itnsource.com/ shotlist/ITN/2012/01/09/T09011225/?v=0&a=0 (accessed 18.3.2013).

13. See C. Griffin, A. Bengry-Howell, C. Hackley, W. Mistral, and I. Szmigin (2009) "The Allure of Belonging: Young Peoples' Drinking Practices and Collective Identification," chapter 11 in M. Wetherell (ed.) *Identity in the 21st Century: New Trends in Changing Times*, pp. 213–230, Palgrave Macmillan, Hampshire; *Identity Studies in the Social Sciences*.

14. Beer ads on TV were full of rugby-types with beards and woolly jumpers sitting in pubs complaining about their "nagging" wives until London ad man John Webster of agency BMP brought the Hofmeister Bear to the screen to sell a watery brand of "lager" beer in the 1980s (http://www.youtube. com/watch?v=LkR0krOm9M4, accessed 19.3.2013). I think this opened up the alcohol market to children-appeal followed by, for example, the cartoon campaigns of, say the Budweiser frogs in the 1990s (http://www.youtube.com/ watch?v=aS3op_7QVIY, accessed 19.3.2013) and on to this 2012 Superbowl ad featuring a dog/barman http://www. youtube.com/watch?v=e_HBagK2ETs (accessed 19.3.2013.)

15. My understanding is that UK alcohol consumption per capita recently fell, but that it has fallen slightly from a historical high as a result of a rising trajectory since the 1960s.

16. http://www.guardian.co.uk/media/2008/dec/17/ofcom-obesity (accessed 19.3.2013).

17. This is one of many examples of investigative journalists exposing the grim reality of the globalised supply chain behind convenience food http://www.guardian.co.uk/ uk/2002/jul/08/bse.foodanddrink (accessed 19.3.2013).

18. See http://www.guardian.co.uk/uk/horsemeat-scandal (accessed 19.3.2013).

19. http://www.guardian.co.uk/society/2012/jun/19/breadline-britain-hungry-schoolchildren-breakfast (accessed 19.3.2013).

20. http://www.tescolotus.net/index_E.php?lang=en (accessed 18.3.2013).

21. See http://www.independent.co.uk/news/business/news/tesco-set-to-admit-defeat-in-dream-to-establish-american-chain-8571899.html (accessed 14.04.2013).

22. See S. Brown (2003) *Free Gift Inside!! Forget the Customer – Develop Marketease*, Chichester, Capstone.

23. See C. Hackley (2003) "How Divergent Beliefs Cause Account Team Conflict," *International Journal of Advertising*, 22, 313– 331. A pre-print of the paper is available at http://www.academia.edu/748052/How_divergent_beliefs_cause_account_team_conflict (accessed 18.3.2013).

24. C. Hackley (2003) "From Consumer Insight to Advertising Strategy: The Account Planner's Integrative Role in Creative Advertising Development" *Marketing Intelligence and Planning*, 21(7), 446–452; C. Hackley (2003) "Divergent Representational Practices in Advertising and Consumer Research: Some Thoughts on Integration," *Qualitative Market Research: An International Journal*, special issue on representation in consumer research, 6(3), 175–184.

## 7   Managing marketing – in context

1. The European tradition of "critical marketing" is where this critique takes place: see, for example, the *Journal of Marketing Management* special issue in 2009, volume 25/7–9, or several books, e.g., M. Tadajewski, P. MacLaran, E. Parsons, and M. Parker (eds) (2011) *Key Concepts in Critical Management Studies*, London, Sage.

2. The notion of marketing as practice has been explored as a counterpoint to the tendency for marketing education to emphasize abstract process categories stripped away from contextual particulars: see, for example, Skålén, P. and Hackley, C. (2011) "Marketing as Practice: Introduction to

the Special Issue," *Scandinavian Journal of Management* 27(2), 189–196; DOI: 10.1016/j.scaman.2011.03.004

3. The template for all marketing text books remains Philip Kotler's 1967 *Marketing Management: Analysis, Planning, Implementation and Control*, 9th edn, New York, Prentice Hall).

4. See http://www.dailymail.co.uk/news/article-2210665/ Vodka-Martini-James-No-thanks-mines-Heineken –just-28-m-worth-product-tie-ins-Skyfall.html (accessed 25.3.2013).

5. Discussed in Douglas Holt's 2004 book *How Brands Become Icons: The Principles of Cultural Branding*, Harvard, MA, Harvard Business School Press.

6. In January 2013, see http://www.guardian.co.uk/media/ table/2013/feb/08/abcs-national-newspapers (accessed 28.3.2013).

7. See http://m.themediabriefing.com/article/2013–03–26/ mail-online-biggest-news-site (accessed 28.3.2013).

8. Source, http://otp.investis.com/clients/uk/dmgt1/rns/regulatory-story.aspx?cid=412&newsid=331387 (accessed 28.3.2013).

9. M. J. Wolf (2003) *The Entertainment Economy: How Mega-Media Forces are Transforming Our Lives*, California, Three Rivers Press.

10. See the Cultural Traction Survey, http://www.culturaltraction.com/the-study/brand-vibe/ (accessed 20.3.2013).

11. For a critique of the notion of "national culture" see B. MacSweeney (2002) "Hofstede's Model of National Cultural Differences and Their Consequences: a Triumph of Faith – a Failure of Analysis," *Human Relations* 55(1), 89–118, article available here http://www.uk.sagepub.com/ managingandorganizations/downloads/Online%20articles/ch05/4%20-%20McSweeney.pdf (accessed 23.3.2013) with an abridged version of the debate on this website: http://geert-hofstede.international-business-center.com/ mcsweeney.shtml (accessed 23.3.2013).

12. For a critical round-up of conventional marketing communications models see C. Hackley (2010) "Theorizing Advertising: Managerial, Scientific and Cultural Appro-

aches," chapter 6 in P. MacLaran, M. Saren, B. Stern, and M. Tadajewski (eds) *The Sage Handbook of Marketing Theory*, London, Sage, pp. 89–107. For an interesting theoretical take on implicit processing of advertisements, and a critique of AIDA-type theories and experimental approaches, see R. Heath (2012) *Seducing the Subconscious – The Psychology of Emotional Influence in Advertising*, Wiley-Blackwell.

13. I touched on the "is-ought" problem some time ago, in one of my first published papers: C. Hackley (1998) "Management Learning and Normative Marketing Theory – Learning from the Life-World," *Management Learning* 29(1), 91–105.

14. P. Bourdieu (1984), *Distinction: A Social Critique of the Judgement of Taste*. London, Routledge.

15. This particular promotion was banned by the UK advertising regulator the ASA since it was judged to be exploitative of children: see the story covered in *Marketing* magazine, http://www.marketingmagazine.co.uk/News/MostEmailed/1170703/Weetabix-online-game-ruled-exploitative-children/ (accessed 23.3.2013).

16. Advergaming is essentially a promotional technique, while online games in general have become marketing brands in themselves. In the UK recently (April 2013) there have been news reports of games that invite players (often children) to download additional power, to "buy gold" or somesuch in order to access higher levels of the game. Unfortunately, this often amounts to the kind of sharp practice that brings marketing into disrepute, because the players are unaware that the account holder is being charged large sums of real money for their upgrades.

17. I'm thinking here of some of the more absurd "the-country's-going-to-hell-in-a-hand-cart" type opinion pieces the *MailOnline* carries that evince both hysterical agreement and contempt in the comment threads.

18. A good account of how marketing studies has used, and abused, theory from sociology, economics and psychology can be found in M. Baker (ed.) (2000) *Marketing Theory: A Student Text*, Cengage Learning.

19. I say more about this in C. Hackley (2009) *Marketing: A Critical Introduction* Sage, London; and in C. Hackley (2003) "'We Are All Customers Now': Rhetorical Strategy and Ideological Control in Marketing Management Texts" *Journal of Management Studies* 40(5), 1325–1352, which is available online in pre-print at http://pure.rhul.ac.uk/portal/en/publications/we-are-all-customers-now-rhetorical-strategy-and-ideological-control-in-marketing-management-texts(e8d66992–7252–4037-ab66-d006ca338862).html (accessed 23.3.2013).

20. For academic perspectives on the theme of proportion in marketing education, see, for example, W. S. Wilkie and E. S. Moore (2003) "Scholarly Research in Marketing; Exploring the 4 Eras of Thought Development," *Journal of Public Policy and Marketing*, 22(Fall), 116–46; and T. H. Witkowski (2005) "Sources of Immoderation and Proportion in Marketing Thought," *Marketing Theory*, 5(2), 221–231.

21. I've done a little bit of investigation into the psychology of expertise, touched upon in this article C. Hackley (1999) "Tacit Knowledge and the Epistemology of Expertise in Strategic Marketing Management," *European Journal of Marketing* 33(7/8), 720–735.

22. An exception might be the use of logarithms that track my web browsing, then send an advertisement for furniture I don't want to my Facebook newsfeed.

23. See R. V. Kozinets (2009) *Netnography- Doing Ethnographic Research Online*, London, Sage.

# Index

Printed and bound by CPI Group (UK) Ltd, Croydon, CR0 4YY